D1561842

THANKS & PRAISE

THANKS & PRAISE

Music Edition

Thanks & Praise is published on behalf of
The Church of Ireland
by Hymns Ancient & Modern Ltd, a registered charity

Hymns Ancient & Modern Ltd
Third Floor, Invicta House
108-114 Golden Lane
London EC1Y 0TG

Thanks & Praise Music Edition
First published September 2015

© 2015 *Compilation*, The Church of Ireland

British Library Cataloguing-in-Publication Data
A catalogue record for this book is available from the British Library.

ISBN 978-1-84825-763-4

Music engraving and typesetting:
Andrew Parker, Ferndown, Dorset BH22 8BB United Kingdom
Printed and bound by CPI Group (UK) Ltd, Croydon CR0 4YY

CONTENTS

GENERAL PREFACE

St Augustine famously said 'to sing is to pray twice.' Both consciously and subconsciously, singing teaches doctrine and builds community. To lift our voices in praise of the Creator of the universe is a joy and a privilege.

The Church of Ireland has a long tradition of hymnody, stretching back to the mid-nineteenth century, when the first edition of *Church Hymnal* was produced (1865). Almost as soon as it was in print there were calls for a wider range of hymns, and a second edition was published just after disestablishment, in 1873, with an appendix added in 1891. The next edition *(CH3)* was produced during and after the First World War and had an appendix added in 1935. The fourth edition *(CH4)* was published in 1960, and its popular supplement *Irish Church Praise* followed in 1990, which in many ways paved the way for the new fifth edition *(CH5)*, launched at the beginning of the new millennium in 2000.

There are all sorts of reasons for such additions to what have been our normative collections of hymnody. Creative hymn- and song-writing continues apace, not least in our day. There is much wonderful and useable material which did not exist when *CH5* was being compiled. A great deal of this material is already in popular use in some churches.

Every collection of hymns proves to have gaps and points where it could be improved. The committee which collated the material to present to General Synod for this supplement was aware of additions which could be made to enhance the Church Hymnal. Some of the key areas include: Lenten material, children's songs, simpler material for baptisms, eucharistic hymns and liturgical material.

It is also true that the popularity of older material rises and wanes. We have therefore added some older hymns and songs which have experienced a revival of late, and which we believe will enhance worship today.

We have also included a range of hymns and liturgical settings in the Irish language, work undertaken in conjunction with Cumann Gaelach na hEaglaise. There are also some new words and music provided by local authors and composers.

When the Hymnal Supplement Committee (a sub-committee of the Liturgical Advisory Committee) invited suggestions for material to be included in the new book, over 1500 items were submitted. Reducing that number of items to a manageable size has been difficult, and invariably there are many worthwhile hymns which space simply would not allow us to include.

Alongside this book and complementing what is already available, Dr Peter Thompson has done the work of providing a *Companion to Thanks & Praise*, and Bishop Edward Darling has completely updated all his work on *Sing to the Word*, which, for many years, has provided help in choosing music to fit the lectionary. Work is also being done to ensure that as much material as possible will be made available as recorded church music.

We wish in particular to express our thanks to the members of the committee: Julie Bell, Alison Cadden, Jacqueline Mullen, Alan Rufli, Derek Verso and the late Donald Davison. We also thank Paul Mullen, David O'Shea, Janet Maxwell, and the staff of Church House, Dublin, who have assisted us in so many ways.

One of the best-known versicles and responses in the *Book of Common Prayer* declares 'O Lord, open our lips ... and our mouth will proclaim your praise.' The praise which comes out of our lips with sincerity can be absolutely infectious. Our prayer is that this latest 'vehicle' of God's praise would be enlivened by the Holy Spirit and bring glory to Jesus Christ. If we don't open our lips and declare his praise, the very stones will sing!

✠ Harold Miller
Editor

MUSICAL PREFACE

Thanks & Praise builds on the variety of material in *Church Hymnal (CH5)*, expanding the range of musical styles. In all singing it is essential to maintain a regular pulse, both within and between verses. Introductions and play-overs are only marked where they are either required by copyright or they are different in some way to the body of the hymn or song. Their function is to establish both tune and tempo, and so they should not be played faster than the pace at which the hymn is to be sung, or have any *rallentando* before the voices begin.

Guitar chords are provided for a wider range of hymns than previously offered, recognising that worship is no longer dependent on a keyboard player, as it was a generation ago. In providing chords the preference has been to give them at pitch rather than using capos, except in keys where the use of a capo would seem the only realistic alternative. Often the guitar chords are not entirely compatible with the keyboard accompaniment, and care should be exercised.

Amongst the metrical hymns, alternative tunes have been suggested whenever there is a particular association between a text and a number of tunes, or whenever a new hymn tune is printed. We hope that many of the new tunes will be explored, learnt and loved, but recognise that there will often be circumstances where a more familiar tune is needed. Many of the alternative tunes suggested are from *CH5*.

In the choice of musical arrangements often we have been bound by the restrictions of copyright holders. Where more freedom has been allowed many new arrangements have been provided to allow greater flexibility in performance. A guiding principle has always been that each item should be performable on a single keyboard instrument, and that the addition of other instruments and percussion should be an enhancement, not a requirement. Many have been arranged with optional parts for choral singing, again to expand the range of possibilities.

Where tunes are already included in *CH5* the opportunity has often been taken to provide a varied arrangement – either in a different key, or in a simplified version. In each case there is a cross-reference and it is hoped that those who have the resources to use the harmony arrangements will consult *CH5*, and equally that when hymns in *CH5* are required in a lower key that musicians will consult *Thanks & Praise*.

Songs from the world church often appear in their original language as well as in English. The original language both conveys the sense of the song, but also forges links across continents, and so congregations are encouraged to explore these in their original context. Many of these were written for unaccompanied singing, in unison or (improvised) harmony, and often benefit from an accompaniment on drums or percussion instruments for a more authentic performance.

A number of rounds have been included in *Thanks & Praise*. Generally short and simple, these are a way of introducing harmony singing to choirs, to Sunday schools and children, and even to entire congregations. They are generally intended for unaccompanied singing, and so a decision was taken not to provide (even optional) accompaniments.

Traditionally in hymnals it is understood that hymns are arranged to be sung in four-part harmony unless marked 'Unison'. In collections of children's, worship and folk songs the opposite often holds true. In *Thanks & Praise* the decision was reached to only denote unison arrangements when they were in the style of a traditional hymn, or when there might be some confusion. Thus many worship songs and much of the children's material, while not marked unison, are arranged for unison singing.

Peter Thompson
Music Editor

Publisher's note

The Publishers thank the owners or controllers of copyright for permission to use the hymns and tunes throughout this collection. Where a copyright text has been altered with permission this is denoted with 'altd.' after the author's name. Acknowledgements are given on-page with the material.

Every effort has been made to trace copyright owners or controllers, to seek permission to use text and music, and to make alterations as necessary. The Publishers apologise to those who have not been traced at the time of going to press, and whose rights have inadvertently not been acknowledged. Any omissions or inaccuracies of permissions or copyright details will be corrected in future printings.

For permission to reproduce copyright hymns and music from this collection, whether in permanent or temporary form, by whatever means, application must be made to the respective owners or controllers.

HYMNS AND SONGS

1

Penlan

76 76 D

Music: David Jenkins (1849–1915)

1 A rich young man came seeking –
    God's kingdom was his aim;
the law had been his guidebook,
    his life was free from blame;
but Jesus asked the courage
    to give his wealth away;
the young man turned in sorrow,
    that price he would not pay.

2 The rich men's gifts were lavish
    and made for public show;
the widow's gift was humble
    and only God would know,
in giving to the Temple,
    although her coins were small,
her gift had so much meaning
    because she gave her all.

3 One boy brought loaves and fishes,
    no other food was there,
but Jesus fed the thousands
    and still had bread to spare;
the miracle of plenty
    soon spread beyond that place;
that simple gift was offered,
    then multiplied by grace.

4 Lord, keep our care for money
    from turning into greed;
help us to use it wisely
    to meet each other's need;
for whether poor or wealthy,
    we have so much to share,
and open-hearted giving
    will show your loving care.

Marjorie Dobson (b. 1940)

2

Immanuel

sign shall be giv - en, a vir - gin will _ con-
(3) what shall be your an - swer? Or will you hear the

- ceive a hu - man ba - by bear - ing un - di -
call of him who did not spare his Son, but

- mi - nished de - i - ty; the glo - ry of the
gave him for us _ all? On earth there is no

Music: Michael Card (*b.* 1957)
　　arranged by Peter Thompson (*b.* 1979)

na - tions, a light for all to see, and
pow - er, there is no depth nor height, could

hope for all who will em - brace his warm re - a - li -
ev - er se - pa - rate us from the love of God in

Optional SATB

Im - ma - nu - el,

- ty.
Christ.

Im - ma - nu - el,

Words: Michael Card (*b.* 1957)

3

Angel voices   85 85 87

Music: Edwin George Monk (1819–1900)

ADVENT 1

1   Advent candles tell their story
      as we watch and pray;
    longing for the day of glory,
      'Come, Lord, soon', we say.
    Pain and sorrow, tears and sadness
      changed for gladness on that day.

ADVENT 2

2   Prophet voices loudly crying,
      making pathways clear,
    glimpsing glory, self-denying,
      calling all to hear.
    Through their message – challenged, shaken –
      hearts awaken: God is near!

ADVENT 3

3   John the Baptist, by his preaching
      and by water poured,
    brought to those who heard his teaching
      news of hope restored:
    'Keep your vision strong and steady,
      and be ready for the Lord.'

ADVENT 4

4   Mary's gift, beyond all telling,
      was to give Christ room.
    She gave God a human dwelling
      in a mother's womb.
    Who could guess the final story?
      – cross and glory; empty tomb!

CHRISTMAS DAY

5   Advent candles tell their story
      on this Christmas Day.
    Those who waited for God's glory:
      they prepared the way.
    Christ is with us; loving, giving,
      in us living, here today!

Mark Earey (b. 1965)

*The prayers overleaf may be used alongside the relevant
verse of this hymn at the candle-lighting.*

Prayers to accompany the preceding hymn

ADVENT 1

God of Abraham and Sarah,
and all the patriarchs of old,
you are our Father too.
Your love is revealed to us in Jesus Christ,
Son of God and Son of David.
Help us in preparing to celebrate his birth
to make our hearts ready for your Holy Spirit
to make his home among us.
We ask this through Jesus Christ,
the light who is coming into the world.
Amen.

ADVENT 2

God our Father,
you spoke to the prophets of old
of a Saviour who would bring peace.
You helped them to spread the joyful message
of his coming kingdom.
Help us, as we prepare to celebrate his birth,
to share with those around us
the good news of your power and love.
We ask this through Jesus Christ,
the light who is coming into the world.
Amen.

ADVENT 3

God our Father,
you gave to Zechariah and Elizabeth in their old age
a son called John.
He grew up strong in spirit,
prepared the people for the coming of the Lord,
and baptized them in the Jordan to wash away their sins.
Help us, who have been baptized into Christ,
to be ready to welcome him into our hearts,
and to grow strong in faith by the power of the Spirit.
We ask this through Jesus Christ,
the light who is coming into the world.
Amen.

ADVENT 4

God our Father,
the angel Gabriel told the Virgin Mary
that she was to be the mother of your Son.
Though Mary was afraid,
she responded to your call with joy.
Help us, whom you call to serve you,
to share like her in your great work
of bringing to our world your love and healing.
We ask this through Jesus Christ,
the light who is coming into the world.
Amen.

CHRISTMAS DAY

God our Father,
today the Saviour is born
and those who live in darkness are seeing a great light.
Help us, who greet the birth of Christ with joy,
to live in the light of your Son
and to share the good news of your love.
We ask this through Jesus Christ,
the light who has come into the world.
Amen.

Common Worship, Times and Seasons

4

The small notes indicate instrumental accompaniment.

All hail the Lamb, enthroned on high;
his praise shall be our battle cry;
he reigns victorious, forever glorious,
his name is Jesus, he is the Lord.

Dave Bilborough (b. 1965)

Music: Dave Bilborough (b. 1965)
  arranged by Julie Bell (b. 1979)

5

1 All heaven de - clares _____ the glo - ry of the
2 I will pro - claim _____ the glo - ry of the

ri - sen Lord. Who can com - pare _____
ri - sen Lord, who once was slain _____

— with the beau - ty of the Lord?
— to re - con - cile __ man to God.

For -ev- er he will be _____ the Lamb up - on the
For -ev- er you will be _____ the Lamb up - on the

The small notes indicate instrumental accompaniment.

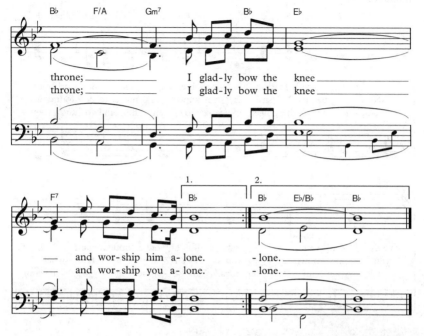

throne; _____ I glad-ly bow the knee _____
throne; _____ I glad-ly bow the knee _____

— and wor-ship him a- lone. - lone. _____
— and wor-ship you a- lone. - lone. _____

Words: Noël Richards (*b.* 1955)
and Tricia Richards (*b.* 1960)

Music: Noël Richards (*b.* 1955) and Tricia Richards (*b.* 1960)
arranged by Julie Bell (*b.* 1979)

6

Knowing you

1 All I once held dear, built my life up - on, all this world re -
2 Now my heart's de - sire is to know you __ more, to be found in
3 Oh, to know the power of your ri - sen __ life, and to know you

- veres, and wars to own, all I once thought gain I have
you and known as yours. To pos - sess by faith what I
in your suf - - fer - ings. To be - come like you in your

count - ed __ loss; spent and worth - less now, com - pared to
could not __ earn, all - sur - pass - ing gift of right - eous-
death, my __ Lord, so with you to live and ne - ver

this:
- ness: *Know - ing you,   Je - sus,   know - ing*
die:

Music: Graham Kendrick (*b.* 1950)

Words: Graham Kendrick (*b.* 1950)

Music: East African Chant
arranged by Geoff Weaver (*b.* 1943) and Michael O'Connor

This is an East African song, and 'Allundé'
means 'Welcome to the new day'

East African Chant

Music: Graham Kendrick (b. 1950)

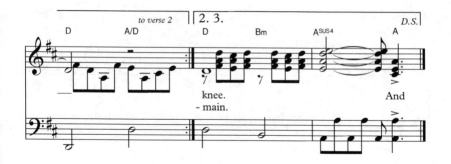

And he shall reign for ever,
his throne and crown shall ever endure.
And he shall reign for ever,
and we shall reign with him.

1   What a vision filled my eyes,
         one like a Son of Man,
     coming with the clouds of heav'n,
         he approached an awesome throne:

2   He was given sovereign power,
         glory and authority;
     every nation, tribe and tongue
         worshipped him on bended knee:

3   On the throne forever,
         see the Lamb who once was slain;
     wounds of sacrificial love
         forever shall remain:

                    Graham Kendrick (b. 1950)

9

Drumrainey

Unison

This tune was originally written for 'Who would think', no. 166.

Music: Peter Thompson (*b.* 1979)

1   As we gather at your table,
      as we listen to your word,
    help us know, O God, your presence,
      let our hearts and minds be stirred.
    Nourish us with sacred story
      till we claim it as our own;
    teach us through this holy banquet
      how to make Love's victory known.

2   Turn our worship into witness
      in the sacrament of life;
    send us forth to love and serve you,
      bringing peace where there is strife.
    Give us, Christ, your great compassion
      to forgive as you forgave;
    may we still behold your image
      in the world you died to save.

3   Gracious Spirit, help us summon
      other guests to share that feast
    where triumphant Love will welcome
      those who had been last and least.
    There no more will envy blind us
      nor will pride our peace destroy,
    as we join with saints and angels
      to repeat the sounding joy.

                          Carl P. Daw, Jr (b. 1944)

9 Words: © Hope Publishing Company, Carol Stream, IL 60188, USA. All rights reserved. Used by permission.

Music: Morris Chapman (*b.* 1948)
    arranged by Peter Thompson (*b.* 1979)

Be bold, be strong,
for the Lord your God is with you;
be bold, be strong,
for the Lord your God is with you!
I am not afraid,
I am not dismayed,
for I'm walking in faith and victory:
come on and walk in faith and victory,
for the Lord your God is with you.

Morris Chapman (b. 1948)

11

Before the throne of God above

DLM extended

1 Be - fore the throne of God a - bove I have a strong, a per-fect plea, a great high priest, whose name is Love, who ev - er lives and pleads for me. My name is writ - ten on his hands, my name is hid - den on his heart; I know that

Music: Vikki Cook (*b.* 1960)

while in heaven he stands no power can force me to de-

-part, no power can force me to de-part.

2 When Satan tempts me to despair
   and tells me of the guilt within,
   upward I look, and see him there
   who made an end of all my sin.
   Because the sinless Saviour died,
   my sinful soul is counted free;
   for God, the just, is satisfied
   to look on him and pardon me,
   to look on him and pardon me.

3 Behold him there, the risen Lamb,
   my perfect, sinless righteousness,
   the great unchangeable I AM,
   the King of glory and of grace!
   One with my Lord I cannot die:
   my soul is purchased by his blood,
   my life is safe with Christ on high,
   with Christ, my Saviour and my God,
   with Christ, my Saviour and my God.

Charitie Lees De Chenez (1841–1923), altd.

12

Verse *(SATB harmony optional)*

1 Be - hold the Lamb who bears our sins a - way, slain for
2 The bo - dy of our Sa - viour, Je - sus Christ, torn for
3 The blood that clean - ses ev - ery stain of sin, shed for
4 And so with thank - ful - ness and faith we rise to re -

Music: Keith Getty (b. 1974), Kristyn Getty (b. 1980)
and Stuart Townend (b. 1963)
arranged by Julie Bell (b. 1979)

1   Behold the Lamb who bears our sins away,
slain for us: and we remember
the promise made that all who come in faith
find forgiveness at the cross.

So we share in this bread of life,
and we drink of his sacrifice,
as a sign of our bonds of peace
around the table of the King.

2   The body of our Saviour, Jesus Christ,
torn for you: eat and remember
the wounds that heal, the death that brings us life,
paid the price to make us one.

3   The blood that cleanses every stain of sin,
shed for you: drink and remember
he drained death's cup that all may enter in
to receive the life of God.

4   And so with thankfulness and faith we rise
to respond and to remember
our call to follow in the steps of Christ
as his body here on earth.

As we share in his suffering,
we proclaim: Christ will come again!
And we'll join in the feast of heaven
around the table of the King.

Keith Getty (b. 1974),
Kristyn Getty (b. 1980)
and Stuart Townend (b. 1963)

13

Music: Keith Getty (*b.* 1974) **and Kristyn Getty** (*b.* 1980)

2 Beneath the cross of Jesus
   his family is my own;
   once strangers chasing selfish dreams,
   now one through grace alone.
   How could I now dishonour
   the ones that you have loved?
   Beneath the cross of Jesus,
   see the children called by God.

3 Beneath the cross of Jesus
   the path before the crown,
   we follow in his footsteps
   where promised hope is found.
   How great the joy before us –
   to be his perfect bride.
   Beneath the cross of Jesus,
   we will gladly live our lives.

Keith Getty (b. 1974)
and Kristyn Getty (b. 1980)

13 Words and Music: © 2005 Thankyou Music. Administered by Capitol CMG Publishing, excl. UK & Europe, administered by Integrity Music, part of the David C Cook family, <songs@integritymusic.com>

14

Slane

1 Bí thu - sa mo shú - ile, a __ Rí mhór __ na __ ndúil, líon __
2 Bí thu - sa mo thre- orú, i __ mbria-thar __ is i mbeart, fan __

thu - sa mo __ bhea - tha __ mo __ chéad-faí's mo __ stuaim; bí
thu - sa go __ deo __ liom, is __ coinn - igh mé __ ceart. __ Glac

thu - sa __ i __ m'a - igne gach oic - he's gach lá, __ im __
cú - ram __ mar __ Ath - air, is éist le mo ghui, __ is tabhair

chod - ladh nó im dhúi - - seacht líon __ mé le do grá.
dom - sa áit __ chó - naí, is - tigh __ i do __ chroí.

14 Harmonisation: © APCK. *See after First Lines index for details.*

1   Bí thusa mo shúile
    a Rí mhóir na ndúil,
    líon thusa mo bheatha
    mo chéadfaí's mo stuaim,
    bí thusa i m'aigne
    gach oíche's gach lá;
    im chodladh nó im dhúiseacht,
    líon mé le do grá.

2   Bí thusa mo threorú
    i mbriathar is i mbeart,
    fan thusa go deo liom
    is coinnigh mé ceart.
    Glac cúram mar Athair
    is éist le mo ghuí,
    is tabhair domsa áit chónaíthe
    istigh i do chroí.

Rop tú mo baile, a Choimdiu cride Irish, 6th
                          century or earlier
              tr. Aodh Ó Dúgain (Hugh Duggan)

Music: Irish traditional melody
    harmonised by George Henry Phillips Hewson (1881–1972)

15

Flowing

Refrain

Bless the Lord, O my soul, O ___ my soul,

wor-ship his ho - ly name. ___ Sing like ne - ver be-fore,

Last time to Coda

O my soul. I'll wor-ship your ho - ly name. ___

Verse *(vv. 2, 3)*

1 The sun comes up, it's a new day dawn-ing;

2   You're rich in love, and you're slow to anger,
     your name is great, and your heart is kind.
     For all your goodness I will keep on singing,
     ten thousand reasons for my heart to find:

Music: Jonas Myrin and Matt Redman (*b.* 1974)

(vv. 2, 3)

A   E   B   C#m

it's time to sing   your song _ a - gain. _ What-

A   E   B

-ev - er may _ pass,   and what - ev - er lies be -

C#m   Aadd9   E   Bsus4   B

- fore me,   let me be sing-ing when the even-ing

3   And on that day when my strength is failing,
the end draws near and my time has come.
Still my soul will sing your praise unending,
ten thousand years and then for evermore:

Jonas Myrin and Matt Redman (*b.* 1974)

Bless the Lord, O my soul, O my soul,
worship his holy name.
Sing like never before, O my soul,
I'll worship your holy name.

1   The sun comes up, it's a new day dawning,
     it's time to sing your song again.
     Whatever may pass, and whatever lies before me,
     let me be singing when the evening comes:

2   You're rich in love, and you're slow to anger,
     your name is great, and your heart is kind.
     For all your goodness I will keep on singing,
     ten thousand reasons for my heart to find:

3   And on that day when my strength is failing,
     the end draws near and my time has come.
     Still my soul will sing your praise unending,
     ten thousand years and then for evermore:

Bless the Lord, O my soul, O my soul,
worship his holy name.
Sing like never before, O my soul.
I'll worship your holy name.

I'll worship your holy name.
Yes, I'll worship your holy name.

                              Jonas Myrin and Matt Redman (*b.* 1974)

16

1 Bless - ed be____ your name in the land that
And bless - ed be____ your name when I'm found in____

____ is plen - ti - ful,____ where your streams of____ a - bun-
____ the de - sert place, though I walk through the wil-

- dance flow, bless-ed____ be your name.
- der - ness, bless-ed____ be your name.

Ev-ery bless-ing you pour out I'll turn back to praise.

And when the dark-ness clo - ses in, Lord, still I will

Music: Matt Redman (b. 1974) and Beth Redman
arranged by Derek Verso (b. 1955)

2   Blessèd be your name
when the sun's shining down on me,
when the world's 'all as it should be',
blessèd be your name.
And blessèd be your name
on the road marked with suffering,
though there's pain in the offering,
blessèd be your name.

give and take a - way, you give and take a -way. My heart will choose to say: Lord, bless-ed be your name. You name. _ Bless-ed be the

1   Blessèd be your name
     in the land that is plentiful,
     where your streams of abundance flow,
     blessèd be your name.
     And blessèd be your name
     when I'm found in the desert place,
     though I walk through the wilderness,
     blessèd be your name.

     Every blessing you pour out I'll
     turn back to praise.
     And when the darkness closes in, Lord,
     still I will say:

Blessèd be the name of the Lord,
blessèd be your name.
Blessèd be the name of the Lord,
blessèd be your glorious name.

2 Blessèd be your name
when the sun's shining down on me,
when the world's 'all as it should be',
blessèd be your name.
And blessèd be your name
on the road marked with suffering,
though there's pain in the offering,
blessèd be your name.

Every blessing you pour out I'll
turn back to praise.
And when the darkness closes in, Lord,
still I will say:

Blessèd be the name of the Lord,
blessèd be your name.
Blessèd be the name of the Lord,
blessèd be your glorious name.

PART TWO:
You give and take away,
you give and take away.
My heart will choose to say:
Lord, blessèd be your name.

Blessèd be the name of the Lord,
blessèd be your name.
Blessèd be the name of the Lord,
blessèd be your glorious name.

Matt Redman (b. 1974)
and Beth Redman

17

Music: Ian Smale (b. 1949)
   arranged by Jacqueline Mullen (b. 1961)

Peace in hea-ven and glo-ry in the high - est; when
mouths stay closed the stones will cry____ out:

D.C. al Fine

(vv. 2,3)

2   Majestic is the King who comes
    in the name of the Lord.
    Majestic is the King who comes
    in the name of the Lord.

3   Triumphant is the King who comes
    in the name of the Lord.
    Triumphant is the King who comes
    in the name of the Lord.

4   Blessèd is the King who comes
    in the name of the Lord.
    Blessèd is the King who comes
    in the name of the Lord.

Ian Smale (*b.* 1949)

18

1 Blest are they, the poor in spi - rit theirs is the
2 Blest are they, the lone - ly ones; _ they shall in -
3 Blest are they _ who show mer - cy; mer - cy

king - dom of God. _ Blest are they, _
- he - rit the earth. _ Blest are they who
shall _ be theirs. _ Blest are they, the

full _ of sor - row; they shall be con - soled. _
hun - ger and thirst; _ they shall have their fill. _
pure _ of heart; _ they _ shall see God. _

Music: David Haas (*b.* 1957)

Vocal arrangement by David Haas (*b.* 1957) and Michael Joncas (*b.* 1951)

adapted by Paul Leddington Wright (*b.* 1951)

1   Blest are they, the poor in spirit;
    theirs is the kingdom of God.
    Blest are they, full of sorrow;
    they shall be consoled.

    Rejoice, and be glad!
    Blessèd are you, holy are you!
    Rejoice and be glad!
    Yours is the kingdom of God!

2   Blest are they, the lowly ones:
    they shall inherit the earth.
    Blest are they, who hunger and thirst;
    they shall have their fill.

3   Blest are they, who show mercy;
    mercy shall be theirs.
    Blest are they, the pure of heart;
    they shall see God!

4   Blest are they, who seek peace;
    they are the children of God.
    Blest are they who suffer in faith;
    the glory of God is theirs.

5   Blest are you, who suffer hate,
    all because of me.
    Rejoice and be glad, yours is the kingdom;
    shine for all to see.

                    David Haas (b. 1957)

19

Grace in essence   65 63

1 Bread is blessed and bro - ken, wine is blessed and
wine _____ is
poured: take this and re - -
blessed and poured: ___
-mem - - ber Christ the Lord.

Music: John L. Bell (b. 1949)

1   Bread is blessed and broken,
        wine is blessed and poured:
    take this and remember
        Christ the Lord.

2   Share the food of heaven
        earth cannot afford:
    here is grace in essence –
        Christ the Lord.

3   Know yourself forgiven,
        find yourself restored,
    meet a friend for ever –
        Christ the Lord.

4   God has kept his promise
        sealed by sign and word:
    here, for those who want him –
        Christ the Lord.

John L. Bell (*b.* 1949)
and Graham Maule (*b.* 1958)

20

Jerusalem

88 88 D (DLM)

1 Bring to the Lord a glad new song child-ren of grace ex-tol your king; wor-ship and praise to God be-long — to in-stru-ments of mu - sic, sing! Let those be

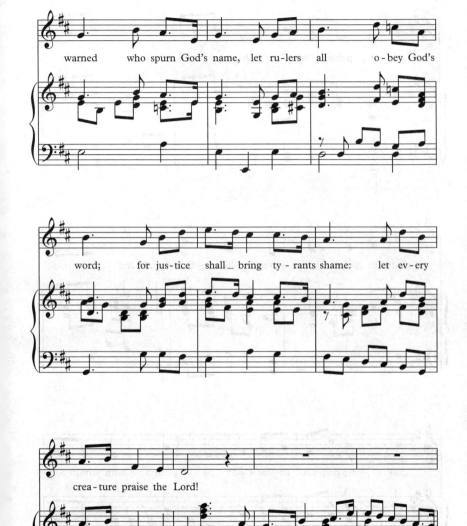

warned   who spurn God's name, let ru-lers   all   o - bey God's

word;   for jus-tice shall _ bring ty - rants shame: let ev - ery

crea - ture praise the Lord!

Music: Charles Hubert Hastings Parry (1848–1918)

2 Sing praise with-in these hal-lowed walls, wor-ship be-

-neath the dome of heaven; by cym-bals' sounds and trum-pets'

calls let prai-ses fit for God be given: with strings and

brass and wind re - joice — then, join our song in full ac -
- cord all liv-ing things with breath and voice; let ev-ery
crea-ture praise the Lord! ____

Words: Michael Perry (1942–1996)
based on Psalms 149 and 150

21

Music: Margaret Rizza (*b.* 1929)

Calm me, Lord, as you calmed the storm;
still me, Lord, keep me from harm.
Let all the tumult within me cease;
enfold me, Lord, in your peace.

David Adam (*b.* 1936)

21 Words: © SPCK Publishing, 36 Causton Street, London SW1P 4ST, UK. Permission applied for.

22

Old Yeavering   87 87

Music: Noël Tredinnick (b. 1949)

1   Child of blessing, child of promise,
       God's you are, from God you came.
    In this sacrament God claims you:
       live as one who bears Christ's name.

2   Child of God, you bear God's image,
       learn to listen for God's call;
    grow to laugh and sing and worship,
       trust and love God more than all.

Ronald S. Cole-Turner (b. 1948)

23

Land of hope and glory

Music: Edward Elgar (1857–1934)
     arranged by Derek Verso (b. 1955)

1   Christ is surely coming, bringing his reward,
     Alpha and Omega, First and Last and Lord:
     Root and Stem of David, brilliant Morning Star:
        meet your judge and Saviour, nations near and far;
        meet your judge and Saviour, nations near and far!

2   See the holy city! There they enter in,
     all by Christ made holy, washed from every sin:
     thirsty ones, desiring all he loves to give,
        come for living water, freely drink, and live;
        come for living water, freely drink, and live!

3   Grace be with God's people! Praise his holy name!
     Father, Son, and Spirit, evermore the same;
     hear the certain promise from the eternal home:
        'Surely I come quickly!'- Come, Lord Jesus, come;
        'Surely I come quickly!'- Come, Lord Jesus, come!

                                Christopher Idle (b. 1938)

Marius

Music: John L. Bell (*b.* 1949)

1 Clap your hands all you nations,
   Amen. Hallelujah!
   shout for joy all you people;
   Amen. Hallelujah!
   holy is the most high;
   Amen. Hallelujah!
   mighty over the earth.
   Amen. Hallelujah!

2 God subdues every nation,
   Amen. Hallelujah!
   God is king of all creatures;
   Amen. Hallelujah!
   God has given this land
   Amen. Hallelujah!
   to the people he loves.
   Amen. Hallelujah!

3 To the shouting in triumph,
   Amen. Hallelujah!
   to the blasting of trumpets,
   Amen. Hallelujah!
   God has gone up,
   Amen. Hallelujah!
   God ascends over all.
   Amen. Hallelujah!

4 Praise the Lord with your singing,
   Amen. Hallelujah!
   sing God psalms for ever,
   Amen. Hallelujah!
   God is monarch of all,
   Amen. Hallelujah!
   sovereign over the earth.
   Amen. Hallelujah!

5 Those on earth who are mighty
   Amen. Hallelujah!
   still belong to our maker,
   Amen. Hallelujah!
   God exalted on high,
   Amen. Hallelujah!
   God forever our Lord.
   Amen. Hallelujah!

John L. Bell (*b.* 1949)
based on Psalm 47

24 Words and Music: From *Psalms of Patience, Protest & Praise*, 1993. © 1993, WGRG, Iona Community, Glasgow G2 3DH Scotland. <www.wgrg.co.uk> All rights reserved. Used by permission.

25

Dundee (French)

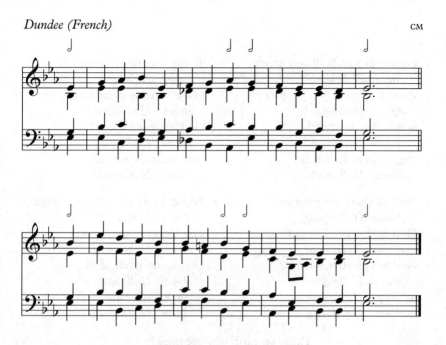

The small notes above the stave indicate an alternative rhythm.
For a full explanation see the 'Musical Preface' to *CH5*, p. xiv.

Music: Melody from the *Scottish Psalter,* 1615
as set in Ravenscroft's *The Whole Booke of Psalmes,* 1621

1   Come, let us use the grace divine,
     and all, with one accord,
in a perpetual covenant join
     ourselves to Christ the Lord:

2   Give up ourselves, through Jesu's power,
     his name to glorify;
and promise, in this sacred hour,
     for God to live and die.

3   The covenant we this moment make
     be ever kept in mind:
we will no more our God forsake,
     or cast his words behind.

4   We never will throw off his fear
     who hears our solemn vow;
and if thou art well pleased to hear,
     come down, and meet us now.

5   To each the covenant blood apply,
     which takes our sins away;
and register our names on high,
     and keep us to that day.

Charles Wesley (1707–1788)

26

Highland Cathedral

10 10 10 10

Unison

Music: Uli Roever and Michael Korb
arranged by Compilers of *Church Hymnary*, 4th edition, 2005

1   Come, Lord, and meet us in this holy hour,
come, Lord and greet us; come to us in power;
    come with refreshment for the weary soul;
    come, Lord, with healing; make the broken whole.

2   Stand then before us as the rite begins;
cleanse and restore us; free us from our sins,
    and, as we contemplate our foolish ways,
    turn all our sadness into joy and praise.

3   Lord, our provider, when the feast is spread,
furnished with wine and everlasting bread,
    fill us with goodness, strengthen us with grace,
    ever enfold us all in love's embrace.

4   Lord, who invites us now to come and dine;
speak through the sacrament of bread and wine,
    and, as we celebrate our Saviour's love,
    fit us for glory in the realms above.

Graham D. S. Deans (b. 1953)

These words were written for the tune ANIMA CHRISTI, *CH5* no. 444.

27

Battle hymn of the republic

77 87 876 with refrain

For another arrangement of this tune see *CH5* no. 113.

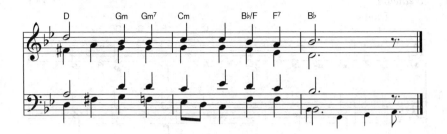

1   Come, sing the praise of Jesus,
      sing his love with hearts aflame,
  sing his wondrous birth of Mary,
      when to save the world he came;
  tell the life he lived for others,
      and his mighty deeds proclaim,
      for Jesus Christ is King.

Praise and glory be to Jesus,
praise and glory be to Jesus,
praise and glory be to Jesus,
   for Jesus Christ is King!

2   There's joy for all who serve him,
      more than human tongue can say;
  there is pardon for the sinner,
      and the night is turned to day;
  there is healing for our sorrows,
      there is music all the way,
      for Jesus Christ is King.

3   To Jesus be the glory,
      the dominion, and the praise;
  he is Lord of all creation,
      he is guide of all our ways;
  and the world shall be his empire
      in the fullness of the days,
      for Jesus Christ is King.

Jack Copley Winslow (1882–1974)

Music: William Steffe *c.* 1852
  arranged by Derek Verso (*b.* 1955)

28

Nettleton

87 87 D

For another arrangement of this tune (suitable for 4-part singing)
in a higher key (D) see no. 157.

Music: American folk melody
arranged by Peter Thompson (b. 1979)

1 Come, thou fount of every blessing,
  tune my heart to sing thy grace;
 streams of mercy never ceasing
  call for songs of loudest praise.
 Teach me some melodious measure
  sung by flaming tongues above;
 O the vast, the boundless treasure
  of my Lord's unchanging love.

2 Here I find my greatest treasure:
  'Hither by thy help I've come',
 and I hope, by thy good pleasure,
  safely to arrive at home.
 Jesus sought me when a stranger,
  wandering from the fold of God;
 he, to save my soul from danger,
  interposed his precious blood.

3 O to grace how great a debtor
  daily I'm constrained to be!
 Let that grace, Lord, like a fetter,
  bind my wandering heart to thee.
 Prone to wander, Lord, I feel it,
  prone to leave the God I love;
 take my heart, O take and seal it,
  seal it from thy courts above!

     Robert Robinson (1735–1790), altd.

29

Morning song (Consolation) 86 86

Music: Early American melody from *Kentucky Harmony,* 1816
harmonised by Peter Thompson (*b.* 1979)

1   Defend me, Lord, from hour to hour,
     and bless your servant's way;
   increase your Holy Spirit's power
     within me day by day.

2   Help me to be what I should be,
     and do what I should do,
   and ever with your Spirit free
     my daily life renew.

3   Grant me the courage from above
     which you impart to all
   who hear your word and know your love
     and answer to your call.

4   So may I daily grow in grace,
     continuing yours alone,
   until I come to sing your praise
     with saints around your throne.

George D'Oyly Snow (1903–1977)

30

Don't build your house on the san - dy land, __ don't build it too near the shore. _____ Well, it may look kind of nice, but you'll have to build it twice, oh, you'll have to build your house once more. You'd bet - ter

* *This song can be sung as a round. Group 2 begins when Group 1 reaches* *

Music: Karen Lafferty (b. 1948)

build your house upon a rock, make a good foun-da-tion on a so-lid spot. Oh, the storms may come and go, but the peace of God you will know.

Words: Karen Lafferty (*b.* 1948)

31

Refrain

Eat this bread, drink this cup, come to him and nev - er be hun - - gry. Eat this bread,

Cantor

2 Our

drink this cup, trust in him and you will not thirst.

Music: Jacques Berthier (1923–1994)

Refrain

Eat this bread, drink this cup, come to him and nev - er be hun - - gry. Eat this bread, drink this cup, trust in him and you will not thirst.

Cantor or group

3 Eat his flesh and drink his blood, and

4 An - y - one who eats this bread will

5 If we be - lieve and eat this bread,

Christ will raise you up on the last day.

live for ev - er.

we will have e - ter - nal life.

Words: Taizé Community
based on John 6

32

Castle Lane

10 10 10 10 10 10

Music: Hugh Benham (b. 1943)

Alternative tune: 145, UNDE ET MEMORES

1   Eternal God, before whose face we stand,
your earthly children, fashioned by your hand,
hear and behold us, for to you alone
all hearts are open, all our longings known:
   so for our world and for ourselves we pray
   the gift of peace, O Lord, in this our day.

2   We come with grief, with thankfulness and pride,
to hold in honour those who served and died;
we bring our hurt, our loneliness and loss,
to him who hung forsaken on the cross;
   who, for our peace, our pains and sorrows bore,
   and with the Father lives for evermore.

3   O Prince of peace, who gave for us your life,
look down in pity on our sin and strife.
May this remembrance move our hearts to build
a peace enduring, and a hope fulfilled,
   when every flag of tyranny is furled
   and wars at last shall cease in all the world.

4   From earth's long tale of suffering here below
we pray the fragile flower of peace may grow,
till cloud and darkness vanish from our skies
to see the Sun of Righteousness arise.
   When night is past and peace shall banish pain,
   all shall be well, in God's eternal reign.

Timothy Dudley-Smith (b. 1926)

33

last time to Coda

Faith as small as a mus - tard seed_ will move moun - tains, move moun - tains. Faith as small as a mus - tard seed_ will move moun - tains by the pow - er of God. God. Be - lieve what Je - sus

Music: Doug Horley
arranged by Dave Bankhead

Faith as small as a mustard seed
will move mountains, move mountains;
faith as small as a mustard seed
will move mountains by the power of God.

(Repeat)

1 Believe what Jesus said was true,
   believe he meant it just for you.
   Wait and see what God will do,
   as you pray, pray, as you pray.

2 Do da do da do da do do da,
   do da do da mountains.
   Do da do da do da do do da,
   do da do da mustard.

Doug Horley

34

Music: Graham Kendrick (*b.* 1950)

Words: Graham Kendrick (b. 1950)

34 Words and Music: © 1996, Graham Kendrick / Make Way Music Ltd, PO Box 320, Tunbridge Wells, Kent. TN2 9DE UK. <www.grahamkendrick.co.uk> Used by permission.

Music: Paul Crouch (*b.* 1963) and David Mudie (*b.* 1961)

1 Father God, you love me and you know me inside out.
You know the words that I will say before I speak them out.
You are all around me, you hold me in your hand.
Your love for me is more than I can ever understand.

2 Father God, from your love there is nowhere I can hide.
If I go down into the depths or cross the ocean wide,
there your love would find me, you'd take me in your hand.
Your love for me is more than I can ever understand.

Paul Crouch (b. 1963) and David Mudie (b. 1961)

36

The Star (An Réalt)

For this tune in a higher key (C) see *CH5* no. 460.

Music: Irish traditional melody
harmonised by George Henry Phillips Hewson (1881–1972)

1   For all your saints in glory, for all your saints at rest,
to you, our Lord and Saviour, all praises be addressed;
apostles, martyrs, prophets, who served you in their day,
have left us their example of following your way.

ST JOSEPH OF NAZARETH – 19 MARCH

2w   We praise you, Christ, for Joseph, a carpenter by fame
who as your earthly father, enriched your holy name.
He taught you faith and wisdom, and nurtured you in mind,
till you became his Master, the Saviour of mankind.

ST PHILIP THE DEACON – 11 OCTOBER

2x   Lord, as your church grew stronger and did become
        well-known
new ministers were needed for loving care alone;
so Philip was commissioned, a deacon kind and true,
who witnessed to your gospel, in loving service too.

ST JAMES, THE BROTHER OF OUR LORD – 23 OCTOBER

2y   Lord, James your earthly brother, became a bishop too,
when knowing you had risen, he placed new faith in you.
Presiding at the council that set the Gentiles free,
he welcomed them as kindred on equal terms to be.

3   All praise to God the Father, all praise to God the Son,
and God the Holy Spirit, eternal Three in One;
till all the ransomed number fall down before the throne,
and honour, power, and glory ascribe to God alone.

vv.2w, 2x Edward F. Darling (*b.* 1933)
v.2y Horatio Bolton Nelson (1823–1913), altd.

These verses supplement hymn 460 in *CH5*.

Music: Keith Getty (b. 1974) and Stuart Townend (b. 1963)

1. From the breaking of the dawn
   to the setting of the sun,
      I will stand on every promise of your word.
   Words of power, strong to save,
   that will never pass away;
      I will stand on every promise of your word.
   For your covenant is sure,
   and on this I am secure:
      I can stand on every promise of your word.

2. When I stumble and I sin,
   condemnation pressing in,
      I will stand on every promise of your word.
   You are faithful to forgive,
   that in freedom I might live,
      so I stand on every promise of your word.
   Guilt to innocence restored;
   you remember sins no more,
      so I'll stand on every promise of your word.

Verses 3 & 4 are found overleaf.

37   Words and Music: © 2005 Thankyou Music. Administered by Capitol CMG Publishing, excl. UK & Europe, administered by Integrity Music, part of the David C Cook family, <songs@integritymusic.com>

me, so I'll stand on ev-ery pro-mise of your

word. 4 Hope that

3   When I'm faced with anguished choice
     I will listen for your voice,
         and I'll stand on every promise of your word.
     Through this dark and troubled land,
     you will guide me with your hand
         as I stand on every promise of your word.
     And you've promised to complete
     every work begun in me,
         so I'll stand on every promise of your word.

4   Hope that lifts me from despair,
     love that casts out every fear
         as I stand on every promise of your word.
     Not forsaken, not alone,
     for the Comforter has come,
         and I stand on every promise of your word.
     Grace sufficient, grace for me,
     grace for all who will believe,
         we will stand on every promise of your word.

Keith Getty (b. 1974)
and Stuart Townend (b. 1963)

38

With a 'celtic' feel

1 From the squa-lor of a bor-rowed sta-ble, by the Spi-rit and a vir-gin's faith; to the an-guish and the shame of scan-dal came the Sa-viour of the hu-man race! But the skies were filled with the praise of heav'n, shep-herds lis-ten as the an-gels tell of the Gift of God come down to man

Music: Stuart Townend (b. 1963)

at the dawn-ing of Im - ma - nu - - el.

2   King of heaven now the friend of sinners,
        humble servant in the Father's hands,
    filled with power and the Holy Spirit,
        filled with mercy for the broken man.
    Yes, he walked my road and he felt my pain,
        joys and sorrows that I know so well;
    yet his righteous steps give me hope again –
        I will follow my Immanuel!

3   Through the kisses of a friend's betrayal,
        he was lifted on a cruel cross;
    he was punished for a world's transgressions,
        he was suffering to save the lost.
    He fights for breath, he fights for me,
        loosing sinners from the claims of hell;
    and with a shout our souls are free –
        death defeated by Immanuel!

4   Now he's standing in the place of honour,
        crowned with glory on the highest throne,
    interceding for his own belovèd
        till his Father calls to bring them home!
    Then the skies will part as the trumpet sounds
        hope of heaven or the fear of hell;
    but the Bride will run to her Lover's arms,
        giving glory to Immanuel!

Stuart Townend (b. 1963)

38 Words and Music: © 1999 Thankyou Music. Administered by Capitol CMG Publishing, excl. UK & Europe, administered by
Integrity Music, part of the David C Cook family, <songs@integritymusic.com>

Music: Elizabeth Estelle White (1925–2011)
  arranged by Derek Verso (b. 1955)

1　Give me peace, O Lord, I pray,
　　in my work and in my play,
　　and inside my heart and mind,
　　　Lord, give me peace.

2　Give peace to the world, I pray,
　　let all quarrels cease today,
　　may we spread your light and love.
　　　Lord, give us peace.

Elizabeth Estelle White (1925–2011)

40

Mount Sion (Pleyel)

88 88 88

Alternative tune: SURREY (CAREY'S), CH5 no. 395.

Music: adapted from a string quartet by Ignacz J. Pleyel
harmonised by Compilers of *Methodist Hymn Book,* 1904

1   Give me the faith which can remove ⌣
        and sink the mountain to a plain;
     Give me the childlike praying love,
        which longs to build thy house again;
     thy love, let it my heart o'erpower,
        and all my simple soul devour.

2   I would the precious time redeem,
        and longer live for this alone:
     to spend, and to be spent, for them
        who have not yet my Saviour known;
     fully on thee my mission prove,
        and only breathe, to breathe thy love.

3   My talents, gifts and graces, Lord,
        into thy blessed hands receive;
     and let me live to preach thy word,
        and let me to thy glory live;
     my every sacred moment spend
        in publishing the sinners' friend.

4   Enlarge, inflame, and fill my heart
        with boundless charity divine:
     so shall I all my strength exert,
        and love them with a zeal like thine;
     and lead them to thy open side,
        the sheep for whom their Shepherd died.

                    Charles Wesley (1707–1788)

40

SECOND TUNE

Clements

88 88 88

Unison

Music: Alison Cadden (*b.* 1965)

1 Give me the faith which can remove
  and sink the mountain to a plain;
Give me the childlike praying love,
  which longs to build thy house again;
thy love, let it my heart o'erpower,
  and all my simple soul devour.

2 I would the precious time redeem,
  and longer live for this alone:
to spend, and to be spent, for them
  who have not yet my Saviour known;
fully on thee my mission prove,
  and only breathe, to breathe thy love.

3 My talents, gifts and graces, Lord,
  into thy blessed hands receive;
and let me live to preach thy word,
  and let me to thy glory live;
my every sacred moment spend
  in publishing the sinners' friend.

4 Enlarge, inflame, and fill my heart
  with boundless charity divine:
so shall I all my strength exert,
  and love them with a zeal like thine;
and lead them to thy open side,
  the sheep for whom their Shepherd died.

Charles Wesley (1707–1788)

41

Highwood

For this tune in a higher key (C) see *CH5* no. 157.

Music: Richard Runciman Terry (1865–1938)

1   Glory to God, the source of all our mission;
      Jesus be praised, the Saviour, Lord and Son!
    Praise to the Spirit who confirms the vision;
      in all the world the will of God be done!

2   Proud in our wealth, or destitute and broken,
      we cannot live by earthly bread alone;
    but by the word that God himself has spoken
      we are set free to make our master known.

3   Eastward or westward, northward, southward moving,
      finding new fields, new patterns and new role,
    Christ's fellow-workers, all his goodness proving,
      see how our God is making people whole!

4   Linked by the cross at which we are forgiven,
      joined by the love that came to find and save,
    one in the hope of God's new earth and heaven,
      we love and give since he first loved and gave.

5   Send us, Lord Christ, to serve at your direction,
      dying and living, yours in loss and gain,
    true to the Gospel of your resurrection,
      working and praying till you come to reign.

Christopher Idle (b. 1938)

42

Diademata

DSM

For this tune in a higher key (E flat) see *CH5* no. 263.

Music: George Job Elvey (1816–1893), altd.

1   Go at the call of God,
       the call to follow on,
to leave security behind
       and go where Christ has gone.
Go in the name of God,
       the name of Christ you bear;
take up the cross, its victim's love
       with all the world to share.

2   Go in the love of God,
       explore its depth and height;
held fast by love that cares, that heals,
       in love walk in the light;
go in the strength of God,
       in weakness prove God true;
the strength that dares to love and serve
       God will pour out in you.

3   Go with the saints of God,
       our common life upbuild,
that daily as we walk God's way
       we may with love be filled;
O God, to you we come,
       your love alone to know,
your name to own, your strength to prove,
       and at your call to go.

Rosalind Brown (b. 1953)

43

Coelites plaudant

11 11 11 5

Unison

Alternative tune: CHRISTE SANCTORUM, *CH5* no. 53

Music: Melody from *Rouen Antiphoner,* 1728
harmonised *by* Ralph Vaughan Williams (1872–1958)

1   God everlasting, wonderful and holy,
Father most gracious, we who stand before thee
here at thine altar, as thy Son has taught us,
    come to adore thee.

2   Countless the mercies thou has lavished on us,
source of all blessing to all creatures living,
to thee we render, for thy love o'erflowing,
    humble thanksgiving.

3   Now in remembrance of our great Redeemer,
dying on Calvary, rising and ascending,
we bring before you what he ever offers,
    sinners befriending.

* 4   Strength to the living, rest to the departed,
grant, holy Father, through Christ's pure oblation;
may the life-giving Bread for ever bring us ‿
    health and salvation.

Harold Riley (1903–2003)

44

Refrain

God loves___ you, and I love___ you, and that's the way ___ it should be. God loves___ you, and I love___ you, and that's the way ___ it should be.

Verse

1 You can be hap - py, and I can be hap - py, and

Music: Anonymous
    arranged by Donald Thomson (*b.* 1968)

that's— the way— it should be.

You can be hap - py, and I can be hap - py, and

that's— the way— it should be.

D.C. al Fine

2   You can be very sad, and I can be very sad,
        that's not the way it should be.
     You can be very sad, and I can be very sad,
        that's not the way it should be, 'cos

3   We can love others like sisters and brothers,
        and that's the way it should be.
     We can love others like sisters and brothers,
        and that's the way it should be.

                                    Anonymous

45

1 Great is___ the dark-ness___ that co - vers___ the earth, op-
2 May now_ your church rise_ with pow - er___ and love, this
3 Great ce - le - bra - tions on that fi - nal day when

-pres - sion, in - jus - tice_ and pain.
glo - ri - ous gos - pel_ pro - claim.
out of___ the hea - vens you come.

Na - tions are slip - ping in hope - less_ des - pair, though
In ev - ery nat - ion_ sal - va - tion_ will come to
Dark - ness will va - nish, all sor - row_ will end, and

Music: Gerald Coates (*b.* 1944) and Noël Richards (*b.* 1955)

Refrain

Come, Lord Je - sus, come, Lord Je - sus, pour out your Spi - rit, we pray, come, Lord Je - sus, come, Lord Je - sus, pour out your Spi - rit on us to - day.

1   Great is the darkness that covers the earth,
oppression, injustice and pain.
Nations are slipping in hopeless despair,
though many have come in your name.
  Watching while sanity dies,
  touched by the madness and lies.

Come, Lord Jesus, come, Lord Jesus,
  pour out your Spirit we pray.
Come, Lord Jesus, come, Lord Jesus,
  pour out your Spirit on us today.

2   May now your church rise with power and love,
this glorious gospel proclaim.
In every nation salvation will come
to those who believe in your name.
  Help us bring light to this world
  that we might speed your return.

3   Great celebrations on that final day
when out of the heavens you come.
Darkness will vanish, all sorrow will end,
and rulers will bow at your throne.
  Our great commission complete,
  then face to face we shall meet.

Gerald Coates (b. 1944)
and Noël Richards (b. 1955)

46

EASTER

Salve festa dies   Irregular

Refrain
Unison

Hail thee, Fes - ti - val Day! blest day that art hal - lowed for

ev - - er; day where - in Christ a - rose, break - ing the

vv. 1, 3

king - dom of death. 1 Lo, the fair beau - ty of earth, from the
                    3 Rise now, O Lord from the grave, and

death of the win - ter a - ris - ing; ev - - ery good
cast off the shroud that en - wrapped thee; leav - ing the _

Music: Ralph Vaughan Williams (1872–1958)

repeat Refrain

gift of the year __ now with the Mas-ter re-turns.
ca-verns of death, show us the light of thy face.

vv. 2, 4

2 Ill it be-seem-eth that thou, by whose hand all __
4 God of all pi-ty and power, let thy word be as-

things are en-com-passed, cap-tive and bound should re-
-sured to the doubt-ing; lo, he breaks forth from the

repeat Refrain

-main, deep in the gloom of the rock. __
tomb! see, he ap-pears to his own! __

Venantius Honorius Clementianus Fortunatus (*c.* 540–early 7th century)
tr. Maurice Frederick Bell (1862–1947), altd.

47

ASCENSION

Salve festa dies

Irregular

Refrain
Unison

Hail thee, Fes - ti - val Day! blest day that art hal-lowed for

ev - - er; day when Christ a - scends, high in the

vv. 1, 3

hea - vens to reign. 1 He who was nailed to the cross is
3 Christ, in thy tri-umph a-scend: thou hast

Lord and the ru - ler of all things; all things cre -
led cap - ti - vi - ty cap - tive; hea - ven her —

Music: Ralph Vaughan Williams (1872–1958)

47 Music: From *The English Hymnal*, 1906, Reproduced by permission of Oxford University Press. All rights reserved.

Venantius Honorius Clementianus Fortunatus (*c.* 540–early 7th century)
v. 1 Maurice Frederick Bell (1862–1947), altd.
and Compilers of *New English Hymnal,* 1986, altd.

48

PENTECOST

Salve festa dies

Irregular

Refrain
Unison

Hail thee, Fes - ti - val Day! blest day that art hal - lowed for

ev - - er; day when the Lord from heaven shone on the

world with his grace.

vv. 1, 3

1 Lo! in the like-ness of fire, on
3 Hark! in a hun - dred _ tongues Christ's

those who a - wait his ap - pear - ing, he whom the _
own, his _ cho - sen a - pos - tles, preach to a _

Music: Ralph Vaughan Williams (1872–1958)

repeat Refrain

Lord fore-told___ sud-den-ly swift-ly a-scends.
hun-dred tribes___ Christ and his won-der-ful works.

vv. 2, 4

2 Forth from the Fa-ther he comes with his seven-fold
4 Praise to the Spi-rit of life, all___ praise to

mys---ti-cal dow---ry, pour-ing on hu-man
fount of our be---ing, light that now light-ens

repeat Refrain

souls in-fi-nite rich--ness of God.___
all, life that in all now a-bides.___

Venantius Honorius Clementianus Fortunatus (*c.* 540–early 7th century)
tr. George Gabriel Scott Gillett (1873–1948)

49

Introduction

Hal-le-lu, hal-le-lu, hal-le-lu, hal-le-lu-jah; we'll praise the Lord! Hal-le-lu, hal-le-lu, hal-le-lu, hal-le-lu-jah; we'll praise the Lord!

We'll praise the Lord, hal-le-lu-jah! We'll praise the Lord, hal-le-lu-jah!

We'll praise the Lord, hal-le-lu-jah! We'll praise the Lord!

49 Arrangement: © Jacqueline Mullen

Hallelu, hallelu, hallelu, hallelujah;
we'll praise the Lord!
Hallelu, hallelu, hallelu, hallelujah;
we'll praise the Lord!
We'll praise the Lord, hallelujah!
We'll praise the Lord, hallelujah!
We'll praise the Lord, hallelujah!
We'll praise the Lord!

Anonymous

Music: Anonymous
    arranged by Jacqueline Mullen (b. 1961)

50

He came down

He came down that we may have love: he

came down that we may have love; he came down that we may

Cantor: Why did he come?

have love; *hal - le - lu - jah for ev - er - more.*

Music: Melody from Cameroon
   transcribed and arranged John L. Bell (b. 1949)

1 He came down that we may have love;
he came down that we may have love;
he came down that we may have love;
hallelujah for evermore.

2 He came down that we may have peace;
he came down that we may have peace;
he came down that we may have peace;
hallelujah for evermore.

3 He came down that we may have joy;
he came down that we may have joy;
he came down that we may have joy;
hallelujah for evermore.

4 He came down that we may have power;
he came down that we may have power;
he came down that we may have power;
hallelujah for evermore.

5 He came down that we may have hope;
he came down that we may have hope;
he came down that we may have hope;
hallelujah for evermore.

Traditional, from Cameroon

He made the stars to shine,
he made the rolling sea,
he made the mountains high,
    and he made me.
But this is why I love him,
for me he bled and died,
the Lord of all creation,
    became the crucified.

Archie Hall (*b.* 1927)

Music: Archie Hall (*b.* 1927)
    arranged by Jacqueline Mullen (*b.* 1961)

52

Music: **Anonymous**
  arranged by **Jacqueline Mullen** (b. 1961)

1   He's got the whole world in his hands,
he's got the whole world in his hands,
he's got the whole world in his hands,
he's got the whole world in his hands.

2   He's got you and me, brother, in his hands,
he's got you and me, brother, in his hands,
he's got you and me, brother, in his hands,
he's got the whole world in his hands.

3   He's got you and me, sister, in his hands,
he's got you and me, sister, in his hands,
he's got you and me, sister, in his hands,
he's got the whole world in his hands.

4   He's got the tiny little baby in his hands,
he's got the tiny little baby in his hands,
he's got the tiny little baby in his hands,
he's got the whole world in his hands.

5   He's got everybody here in his hands,
he's got everybody here in his hands,
he's got everybody here in his hands,
he's got the whole world in his hands.

Anonymous

53

Celeste

LM

Music: Lancashire Sunday School Songs, 1857

1   How good is the God we adore,
        our faithful, unchangeable friend
    whose love is as great as his power,
        and knows neither measure nor end!

2   For Christ is the first and the last,
        his Spirit shall guide us safe home;
    we'll praise him for all that is past,
        and trust him for all that's to come.

Joseph Hart (1712–1767)

54

Faughan Side

86 86 D

Music: Irish traditional melody
arranged by Julie Bell (*b.* 1979)

1   How lovely is your dwelling place,
        O Lord of hosts, to me;
     my soul is longing and fainting ⌣
        the courts of the Lord to see.
     My heart and flesh, they are singing ⌣
        for joy to the living God.
     How lovely is your dwelling-place,
        O Lord of hosts, to me.

2   Even the sparrow finds a home
        where he can settle down;
     and the swallow she can build a nest
        where she may lay her young;
     within the court of the Lord of hosts,
        my King, my Lord and my God;
     and happy are those who are dwelling where ⌣
        the song of praise is sung.

Verses 3 & 4 are found overleaf.

THANKS & PRAISE

3 And I'd rather be a door-keeper
   and only stay a day,
than live the life of a sinner
   and have to stay away;
for the Lord is shining as the sun,
   and the Lord, he's like a shield;
and no good thing does he withhold ⌣
   from those who walk his way.

4 How lovely is your dwelling place,
   O Lord of hosts, to me;
my soul is longing and fainting ⌣
   the courts of the Lord to see;
my heart and flesh, they are singing ⌣
   for joy to the living God.
How lovely is your dwelling-place,
   O Lord of hosts, to me.

Jonathan Asprey (*b.* 1949)
based on Psalm 84

55

Nunc dimittis   667 667

How sa-cred is this place! Its o-pen door of grace,

be bold, my soul to en - ter! May all who wor-ship here,

be - liev-ing God is near, find God is at the cen - tre.

Music: Melody for *Nunc dimittis*
in *Pseaulmes cinquante de David,* Lyons, 1547
Louis Bourgeois (*c.* 1510–1561)
harmony chiefly by Claude Goudimel (*d.* 1572)

How sacred is this place!
Its open door of grace,
  be bold, my soul, to enter!
May all who worship here,
believing God is near,
  find God is at the centre.

Fred Pratt Green (1903–2000)

56

Ombersley

LM

Music: William Henry Gladstone (1840–1891)

1   'How shall they hear', who have not heard ⌣
    news of a Lord who loved and came;
nor known his reconciling word,
    nor learned to trust a Saviour's name?

2   'To all the world', to every place,
    neighbours and friends and far-off lands,
preach the good news of saving grace;
    go while the great commission stands.

3   'Whom shall I send?' who hears the call,
    constant in prayer, through toil and pain,
telling of one who died for all,
    to bring a lost world home again?

4   'Lord, here am I', your fire impart ⌣
    to this poor cold self-centred soul;
touch but my lips, my hands, my heart,
    and make a world for Christ my goal.

5   Spirit of love, within us move:
    Spirit of truth, in power come down!
So shall they hear and find and prove
    Christ is their life, their joy, their crown.

Timothy Dudley-Smith (b. 1926)

57

My Saviour's love

87 87 with refrain

1 I stand a-mazed in the pre - sence of Je - sus the Na - za -rene, and won - der how he could love me, a sin - ner, con - demned, un - clean.

Refrain

O, how mar - vel- lous! O, how won - der- ful, and my song shall ev - er be:

Music: Charles Hutchinson Gabriel (1856–1932)

2   For me it was in the garden
        he prayed – 'Not my will, but thine';
    he shed both tears for his own griefs,
        and sweat-drops of blood for mine.

3   In pity angels beheld him,
        and came from the world of light
    to comfort him in the sorrows
        he bore for my soul that night.

4   He took my sins and my sorrows,
        he made them his very own;
    he bore my burden to Calvary,
        and suffered and died alone.

5   When with the ransomed in glory
        his face I at last shall see,
    my joy will be through the ages
        to sing of his love for me.

Charles Hutchinson Gabriel (1856–1932), altd.

I will not be a-fraid of what I hear, — I will
not be a-fraid of what I see, — I will not be a-fraid of
a - ny - thing — 'cos I know God's with me. —

I will not be afraid of what I hear,
I will not be afraid of what I see,
I will not be afraid of anything
'cos I know God's with me.

1   Like Moses on the mountain,
        or Paul upon the sea,
    or John the Baptist speaking out,
        I know that God's with me.

2   Like Mary with the angel,
        or Peter when set free,
    or David hiding in a cave,
        I know that God's with me.

3   Like Noah in the flooding,
        or Joshua's victory,
    or Esther standing up for truth,
        I know that God's with me.

                                        Nick Harding

Music: Nick Harding

59

Verse

1 I will of-fer up my life in spi-rit and truth,
2 You de-serve my ev-ery breath for you've paid the great cost;

— pour-ing out the oil of love as my wor-ship to you.
— giv-ing up your life to death, e-ven death on a cross.

— In sur-ren-der I must give my ev-ery part;
— You took all my shame a-way, there de-feat-ed my sin,

— Lord, re-ceive the sa-cri-fice of a bro-ken heart.
— o-pened up the gates of heaven, and have beck-oned me in. —

Music: Matt Redman (*b.* 1974)

Refrain

Jesus, what can I give, ___ what can I bring

to so faithful a friend, ___ to so loving a King?

Saviour, what can be said, ___ what can be sung

as a praise of your name ___ for the things you have done?

1   I will offer up my life
      in spirit and truth,
pouring out the oil of love
      as my worship to you.
In surrender I must give
      my every part;
Lord, receive the sacrifice
      of a broken heart.

    Jesus, what can I give, what can I bring
      to so faithful a friend, to so loving a King?
    Saviour, what can be said, what can be sung
      as a praise of your name for the things you have done?
    Oh, my words could not tell, not even in part,
      of the debt of love that is owed by this thankful heart.

2   You deserve my every breath
      for you've paid the great cost;
giving up your life to death,
      even death on a cross.
You took all my shame away,
      there defeated my sin,
opened up the gates of heaven,
      and have beckoned me in.

Matt Redman (*b.* 1974)

60

Calon Lân

87 87 D

Alternative tune: HYFRYDOL, *CH5* no. 493

Music: John Hughes (1872–1914)
 arranged by Peter Thompson (b. 1979)

1   I will sing the wondrous story
      of the Christ who died for me;
   how he left his home in glory
      for the cross of Calvary:

   Yes, I'll sing the wondrous story
      of the Christ who died for me;
   sing it with the saints in glory,
      gathered by the crystal sea.

2   I was lost but Jesus found me,
      found the sheep that went astray;
   threw his loving arms around me,
      drew me back into his way.

3   Days of darkness still come o'er me;
      sorrow's paths I often tread,
   but the Saviour still is with me;
      by his hand I'm safely led.

4   He will keep me till the river
      rolls its waters at my feet;
   then he'll bear me safely over,
      where the loved ones I shall meet.

Francis Harold Rowley (1854–1952)

61

Allegro (♩ = 120)

Unison

1 I'll go in the strength of the Lord,
2 I'll go in the strength of the Lord,
3 I'll go in the strength of the Lord,

in paths he has marked for my
to work he ap - points me to
to con - flicts which faith will re -

Music: Ivor Bosanko (*b.* 1935)

full - ness my wants — shall sup - ply; on
power my suf - fi - cien - cy prove; I'll
meet and en - coun - ter the foe, with

him, till my jour - ney shall end, my un -
trust his om - ni - po - tent arm and —
his sword of truth — in my hand, to —

-wa - ver - ing faith — shall re - ly: —
prove his un - change - ab - le love: —
suf - fer and tri - umph I'll go: —

1   I'll go in the strength of the Lord,
        in paths he has marked for my feet;
    I'll follow the light of his word,
        nor shrink from the dangers I meet.
    His presence my steps shall attend,
        his fullness my wants shall supply;
    on him, till my journey shall end,
        my unwavering faith shall rely.

I'll go (I'll go) I'll go in the strength,
* I'll go in the strength of the Lord.*
I'll go (I'll go) I'll go in the strength,
* I'll go in the strength of the Lord.*

2   I'll go in the strength of the Lord
        to work he appoints me to do;
    in joy which his smile doth afford
        my soul shall her vigour renew.
    His wisdom shall guard me from harm,
        his power my sufficiency prove;
    I'll trust his omnipotent arm,
        and prove his unchangeable love.

3   I'll go in the strength of the Lord
        to conflicts which faith will require;
    his grace as my shield and reward,
        my courage and zeal shall inspire.
    Since he gives the word of command,
        to meet and encounter the foe,
    with his sword of truth in my hand,
        to suffer and triumph I'll go.

Edward Turney (1816–1872)

62

Be happy

Lively

I'm gon-na jump up and down, gon-na spin right a-round, gon-na praise your name for-ev - er. I'm gon-na shout out loud, gon-na deaf-en the crowd, gon-na send my praise to hea - ven. I'm gon-na - ven. I will run this race and I will ne-ver

Music: Doug Horley (*b.* 1953)

Words: **Doug Horley** (b. 1953)

63

At the Cross

This may be sung to JACKSON (BYZANTIUM), *CH5* no. 116, omitting the refrain.

Music: Ralph Erskine Hudson (1843–1901)

faith   I re-ceived my _ sight, and   now   I am hap-py all the day.

1   I'm not ashamed to own my Lord,
        or to defend his cause;
    maintain the honour of his word,
        the glory of his cross.

    At the cross, at the cross, where I first saw the light,
        and the burden of my heart rolled away;
    it was there by faith I received my sight,
        and now I am happy all the day.

2   Jesus, my God! I know his name
        his name is all my trust:
    nor will he put my soul to shame,
        nor let my hope be lost.

3   Firm as his throne his promise stands;
        and he can well secure
    what I've committed to his hands,
        till the decisive hour.

4   Then will he own my worthless name
        before his Father's face;
    and, in the new Jerusalem,
        appoint my soul a place.

verses Isaac Watts (1674–1748)
refrain Ralph Erskine Hudson (1843–1901)

Music: Stuart Townend (*b.* 1963) and Keith Getty (*b.* 1974)

2   In Christ alone! – who took on flesh,
      fullness of God in helpless babe!
This gift of love and righteousness,
      scorned by the ones he came to save:
till on that cross as Jesus died,
      the wrath of God was satisfied –
for every sin on him was laid;
      here in the death of Christ I live.

3   There in the ground his body lay,
      light of the world by darkness slain:
then bursting forth in glorious day
      up from the grave he rose again!
And as he stands in victory,
      sin's curse has lost its grip on me,
for I am his and he is mine –
      bought with the precious blood of Christ.

4   No guilt in life, no fear in death,
      this is the power of Christ in me;
from life's first cry to final breath,
      Jesus commands my destiny.
No power of hell, no scheme of man,
      can ever pluck me from his hand;
till he returns or calls me home,
      here in the power of Christ I'll stand!

Stuart Townend (b. 1963)
and Keith Getty (b. 1974)

65

Refrain
Unison

In the heart__ where__ love is a - bid - ing, God is in that heart.
U - bi ca - ri - tas et a - mor__ De - us i - bi est.

Verse

1 And the love__ of__ Christ has made us__ all of one heart.
2 May no quar - rel - ing or dis - pute__ come be - tween us.

Then with joy - ful__ and with glad__ hearts__ let us thank him.
Let us see__ your__ face O Lord__ Christ, now a - mong us.

Let us fear God__ and re - mem - ber__ all his good - ness.
Let us sing with__ all the an - gels__ praise to Je - sus.

Let us love each o-ther with a pure and clean heart.
In a song of joy that wells up from a clean heart.

In the heart where love is abiding, God is in that heart.
(Ubi caritas et amor Deus ibi est.)

1   And the love of Christ has made us all of one heart.
    Then with joyful and with glad hearts let us thank him.
    Let us fear God and remember all his goodness.
    Let us love each other with a pure and clean heart.

2   May no quarreling or dispute come between us.
    Let us see your face, O Lord Christ, now among us.
    Let us sing with all the angels praise to Jesus.
    In a song of joy that wells up from a clean heart.

Paul Wigmore (1925–2014)
based on *Ubi caritas* from the liturgy of Maundy Thursday

Music: Mode vi, 10th century or earlier
    adapted by Peter Thompson (b. 1979)

Cantor

1 You are my sal - va - - tion;

2 The Lord is my

3 I call up - on the Lord God who is

4 My soul shall sing to

5 With joy you will draw wa - - ter at the

Ostinato

Dm C F F/A B♭ C Dm C

In the Lord I'll be ev - er thank - ful, in the

Music: Jacques Berthier (1923–1994)

I trust in you. I shall not be a--
rock. The Lord is my fort - ress.
wor - thy of praise.
you; you have done won-drous things, O
foun - tain of sal - va - tion. Give
Lord I will re - joice! Look to God, do not be a-

66 Words and Music: © 1998, Ateliers et Presses de Taizé, 71250 Taizé, France

-fraid, you are my strength;

My God, you are my

The Lord shall

God. Let this be known, let this be

thanks to the Lord.

Dm   C   F   B♭6   C   Am

fraid. Lift up your voi - ces, the Lord is near; ___ lift up your

you are my song.

re - - - fuge and my shield.

save _____ me.

known through - - out the world.

Pro - claim God's name.

voi - - ces, the Lord is near.

Words: Taizé Community
based on Isaiah 12:2-6, Psalm 18:2-3

67

Kenilworth Place   87 87 87

Alternative tune: GRAFTON, *CH5* no. 241 (second tune)

Music: John Crothers (b. 1948)

1   In the name of Christ we gather,
        in the name of Christ we sing!
    Celebrate new vows, new promise
        of a life's whole offering,
    here ordained to lead God's people
        at the Gospel's beckoning.

2   Sons and daughters of the Spirit –
        these are called to teach and care,
    called as were the first disciples,
        commonwealth of Christ to share,
    by the bread and wine and water
        sacraments of grace declare.

3   In the ministry of preaching
        may the Word spring into life,
    in the time of doubt and challenge
        may its truth affirm belief,
    in the day of pain and darkness
        heal the hurt of guilt and grief.

4   Now within this solemn moment
        we invoke the power of God –
    by the hands laid on in blessing
        be there strength to take the load,
    be there faithfulness in loving,
        be there courage for this road.

5   Word of joy, enlivening Spirit,
        more than lover, parent, friend,
    born in Jesus, born in Mary,
        born in us, that love extend,
    grow within your chosen servant,
        life of God that has no end!

                         Shirley Erena Murray (b. 1931)

68

Jesu tawa pano 66 69

Version for Shona text

Version for English text

Music: Patrick Matsikenyiri (*b.* 1937)

Jesu, tawa pano;
Jesu, tawa pano;
Jesu, tawa pano;
   tawa pano mu zita renyu.

Jesus, we are here;
Jesus, we are here;
Jesus, we are here;
   we are here for you.

Shona original
Patrick Matsikenyiri (*b.* 1937)

Verses can be created and selected as appropriate.

69

Music: Michael Frye (b. 1965)
arranged by Julie Bell (b. 1979)

Words: Michael Frye (*b.* 1965)

70

Once again

1 Je - sus Christ, I think up - on your sac - ri - fice;
2 Now you are ex - alt - ed to the high - est place,

you be - came no - thing, poured out to death. Ma - ny times I've
King of the hea - vens, where one day I'll bow. But for now, I

won - dered at your gift of life, and I'm in that place once a - gain,
mar - vel at this sav - ing grace, and I'm full of praise once a - gain;

Refrain

I'm in that place once a - gain. *And*
I'm full of praise once a - gain.

Music: Matt Redman (b. 1974)

once a-gain I look up-on the cross where you died, — I'm

hum-bled by your mer-cy and I'm bro-ken in-side. —

Once a-gain I thank you, once a-gain I pour out my life. —

3 Thank you for the cross, thank you for the cross,

thank you for the cross, my friend. friend. And

Words: Matt Redman (*b.* 1974)

71

Noël nouvelet

Unison

II II IO II

For another arrangement of this tune see *CH5* no. 278.

Music: French carol
arranged by **Derek Verso** (*b.* 1955)

71 Arrangement: © Derek Verso

1   Jesus Christ is waiting,
     waiting in the streets;
  no one is his neighbour,
     all alone he eats.
  Listen, Lord Jesus,
     I am lonely too.
  Make me, friend or stranger,
     fit to wait on you.

2   Jesus Christ is raging,
     raging in the streets,
  where injustice spirals
     and real hope retreats.
  Listen, Lord Jesus
     I am angry too.
  In the Kingdom's causes
     let me rage with you.

3   Jesus Christ is healing,
     healing in the streets;
  curing those who suffer,
     touching those he greets.
  Listen, Lord Jesus,
     I have pity too.
  Let my care be active,
     healing, just like you.

4   Jesus Christ is dancing,
     dancing in the streets,
  where each sign of hatred
     he, with love, defeats.
  Listen, Lord Jesus
     I should triumph too.
  Where good conquers evil
     let me dance with you.

5   Jesus Christ is calling,
     calling in the streets,
  'Who will join my journey?
     I will guide their feet.'
  Listen, Lord Jesus,
     let my fears be few.
  Walk one step before me;
     I will follow you.

John L. Bell (*b.* 1949)
and Graham Maule (*b.* 1958)

Music: Wendy Churchill (*b.* 1957)

1   Jesus is King and I will extol him,
    give him the glory, and honour his name;
    he reigns on high, enthroned in the heavens –
    Word of the Father, exalted for us.

2   We have a hope that is steadfast and certain,
    gone through the curtain and touching the throne;
    we have a priest who is there interceding,
    pouring his grace on our lives day by day.

3   We come to him, our priest and apostle,
    clothed in his glory and bearing his name,
    laying our lives with gladness before him –
    filled with his Spirit we worship the King:

4   'O holy One, our hearts do adore you;
    thrilled with your goodness we give you our praise!'
    Angels in light with worship surround him,
    Jesus, our Saviour, for ever the same.

Wendy Churchill (b. 1957)

73

Near the Cross

75 75 with refrain

In the cross, in the cross, be my glo - ry ev - er;

till my rap - tured soul shall find rest be-yond the ri - ver.

Music: William Howard Doane (1832–1916)

1   Jesus, keep me near the cross;
      there a precious fountain,
    free to all, a healing stream,
      flows from Calvary's mountain.

In the cross, in the cross,
    be my glory ever;
till my raptured soul shall find
    rest beyond the river.

2   Near the cross, a trembling soul,
      love and mercy found me;
    there the bright and morning star
      shed its beams around me.

3   Near the cross: O Lamb of God,
      bring its scenes before me;
    help me walk from day to day,
      with its shadow o'er me.

4   Near the cross I'll watch and wait,
      hoping, trusting ever,
    till I reach the golden strand,
      just beyond the river.

Frances Jane van Alstyne (Fanny Crosby)
(1820–1915)

74

Al - le - lu - ia, al - le - lu - ia,

As we come with awe and glad - ness,

Je - sus, lead us to the Fa - ther by your Spi - rit,

help us _ draw near. _

help us _ draw near. _

help us _ draw near. _

Music: **Sam Hargreaves** (*b.* 1979)

Al - le - lu - ia, al - le - lu - ia,

As we come with awe and glad - ness,

Je - sus, lead us to the Fa - ther by your Spi - rit,

help us __ draw near. __

help us __ draw near. __

help us __ draw near. __

Words: Sam Hargreaves (b. 1979)

This is a cumulative round. Part 1 sings first, then is joined by part 2. Finally all three parts sing together.

75

1 Jesu's love is very wonderful,
   Jesu's love is very wonderful,
   Jesu's love is very wonderful,
      O wonderful love!

2 So high you can't get over it,
   so low you can't get under it,
   so wide you can't get round it,
      O wonderful love!

(Repeat verse 1.)

H. W. Rattle

Music: Anonymous
   arranged by Jacqueline Mullen (b. 1961)

Stabat Mater

1   Jesus on the cross is dying;
    soon his body will be lying
    in the darkness of the tomb.

2   God's own mother, purest maiden,
    see the sinless One sin-laden,
    blessèd fruit of blessèd womb.

3   Mary's heart for him is aching,
    as she sees her Son's heart breaking
    so that love may be revealed.

4   Now at last her heart is feeling
    sorrow's sword, her Son revealing
    thoughts in many hearts concealed.

Music: Mäyntzisch Gesangbuch, 1661
      adapted by Samuel Webbe, *the elder* (1740–1816)
      Original version from *An Essay ... [on] the Church Plain Chant,* 1799
      harmonised by Andrew Parker (*b.* 1950)

5   How could pity not awaken
for the Son of God, forsaken
    in the loneliness of death?

6   Who would not give consolation
in this mother's desolation
    as he breathes his dying breath?

7   Mary's heart for him is bleeding;
in his blood for sinners pleading,
    God's new law of love is sealed.

8   'It is done', she hears him crying
at the moment of his dying:
    death by death has now been healed.

9   Let my heart with love be burning
for my wounded Jesus, yearning
    for the vision of his face.

10   Let me stand beside you, sharing
grief for Jesus, my sins bearing
    on the cross of Calvary.

11   Let me bear the wounds of Jesus,
drink the precious blood that frees us,
    glory only in his cross.

12   Let the cross be my salvation,
Jesus' death my consolation,
    in that hour when I must die.

James Quinn, SJ (1919–2010)

77

Saranam   Irregular

Je - sus, Sav - iour,

Lord, now to you I fly; sa - ra - nam, sa - ra - nam, sa - ra -

-nam. You're my Rock, my Re - fuge, that's higher than I; sa - ra -

-nam, sa - ra - nam, sa - ra - nam.   1 From my e - ne - mies to

you I flee, from the ends of earth wher - ev - er

Music: Indian melody
         arranged by Geoff Weaver (b. 1943)

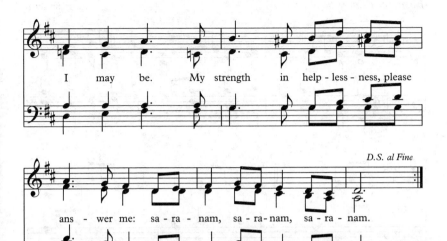

D.S. al Fine

I may be. My strength in help - less - ness, please ans - wer me: sa - ra - nam, sa - ra - nam, sa - ra - nam.

2   In your tent give me a dwelling place,
and beneath your wings may I find sheltering grace,
and may I feel the sunshine of your face:
    saranam, saranam, saranam.

3   May I keep my vows to you each day
and depend upon your love along the way,
and on your faithful strength my burdens lay:
    saranam, saranam, saranam.

4   Yesterday, today, for e'er the same,
Lord you give your grace to all who bear your name;
you ransomed us from sin and took the blame:
    saranam, saranam, saranam.

'Saranam' means 'Refuge'.

Sri Lankan text
tr. Daniel Thambyrajah Niles (1908–1970)
and Compilers of *Church Hymnary Fourth Edition,* 2005
based on Psalm 61

78

Ebenezer (Ton-y-botel)

87 87 D

1 Jesus, tempted in the desert,
    lonely, hungry, filled with dread:
'Use your power,' the tempter tells him;
    'turn these barren rocks to bread!'
'Not alone by bread', he answers,
    'can the human heart be filled.
Only by the Word that calls us
    is our deepest hunger stilled!'

2 Jesus, tempted at the temple,
    high above its ancient wall:
'Throw yourself from lofty turret;
    angels wait to break your fall!'
Jesus shuns such empty marvels,
    feats that fickle crowds request:
'God, whose grace protects, preserves us,
    we must never vainly test.'

3 Jesus, tempted on the mountain
    by the lure of vast domain;
'Fall before me! Be my servant!
    Glory, fame you're sure to gain!'
Jesus sees the dazzling vision,
    turns his eyes another way:
'God alone deserves our homage!
    God alone will I obey!'

4 When we face temptation's power,
    lonely, struggling, filled with dread,
Christ, who knew the tempter's hour,
    come and be our living bread.
By your grace, protect, preserve us
    lest we fall, your trust betray.
Yours, above all other voices,
    be the Word we hear, obey.

Herman G. Stuempfle, Jr (1923–2007)

Music: Thomas John Williams (1869–1944)
    adapted from the anthem Golau yn y Glyn (Light in the Valley)

79

Music: African American traditional
arranged by Julie Bell (b. 1979)

bat-tle of Je-ri - cho, __ and the walls came a-tumb - ling

down. 1 You may talk of your men of Gi-de-on, ___
to the __ walls of Je-ri-cho ___

__ you may talk of your men of Saul, but there's
__ he __ marched with __ spear in hand, 'Go __

Joshua fought the battle of Jericho, Jericho, Jericho,
Joshua fought the battle of Jericho,
and the walls came a-tumbling down.

1   You may talk of your men of Gideon,
      you may talk of your men of Saul,
      but there's none like good old Joshua,
        and the battle of Jericho:

2   Up to the walls of Jericho
      he marched with spear in hand,
      'Go blow them rams' horns,' Joshua cried,
        'for the battle is in my hand.'

3   Then the ram-sheep horns began to blow,
      trumpets began to sound;
      Joshua commanded the people to shout,
        and the walls came a-tumbling down
          that morning …

African American traditional

Music: Jarrod Cooper (b. 1970)

throne. *Your ma - jes - ty,* *I can but bow,* *I lay my*
praise.

all *be -fore you now.* *In roy - al robes* *I don't de-*

-serve *I live to serve* *your ma - jes - ty.* 2 Earth and

- ty, *I live to serve* *your ma - jes - ty.*

Words: Jarrod Cooper (*b.* 1970)

81

Pershore Abbey   66 66 44 44

Alternative tune: DARWALL'S 148TH, *CH5* no. 376

Music: Peter Thompson (*b.* 1979)

1   Let all creation dance
        in energies sublime,
    as order turns with chance,
        unfolding space and time;
            for nature's art
            in glory grows,
            and newly shows
        God's mind and heart.

2   God's breath each force unfurls,
        igniting from a spark
    expanding starry swirls,
        with whirlpools dense and dark.
            Though moon and sun
            seem mindless things,
            each orbit sings:
        'Your will be done'.

3   Our own amazing earth,
        with sunlight, cloud and storms,
    and life's abundant growth
        in lovely shapes and forms
            is made for praise,
            a fragile whole,
            and from its soul
        heaven's music plays.

4   Lift heart and soul and voice:
        in Christ all praises meet,
    and nature shall rejoice
        as all is made complete.
            In hope be strong,
            all life befriend,
            and kindly tend
        creation's song.

                        Brian Wren (b. 1936)

82

Christmas calypso

1 Let me tell you a-bout a ba-by, and his fa-mi-ly. It is writ-ten down in the Bi-ble so you might be-lieve. Ma-ny men had told of his com-ing down through his-to-ry.

2 There was once a young girl
  called Mary,
  only in her teens.
She was visited by an angel,
  sent to Galilee.
And he told her she'd have a baby,
  how she couldn't see.
Yet it was her will to obey him,
  so it was agreed.

3 Well, in those days Caesar Augustus
  issued a decree,
and so Mary went with her husband
  where they had to be.
There was nowhere else but a stable,
  where they both could sleep.
It was there that she had her baby,
  born for you and me.

Mark Johnson
and Helen Johnson

Music: Mark Johnson and Helen Johnson
    arranged by Paul Leddington Wright (b. 1951)

83

Linstead market

LM with refrain

Unison

Refrain

Je - sus lives a - gain, earth can breathe a-gain, pass the word a-round: loaves a-bound!

Music: Jamaican traditional melody
arranged by Ethel Olive Doreen Potter (1925–1980)

1   Let us talents and tongues employ,
     reaching out with a shout of joy:
          bread is broken, the wine is poured,
          Christ is spoken and seen and heard.

     Jesus lives again, earth can breathe again,
     pass the Word around: loaves abound!

2   Christ is able to make us one,
     at the table he sets the tone,
          teaching people to live to bless,
          love in word and in deed express.

3   Jesus calls us in – sends us out
     bearing fruit in a world of doubt,
          gives us love to tell, bread to share:
          God (Immanuel!) everywhere.

                                        Fred Kaan (1929–2009)

84

Zechariah

76 76 D

Music: Theodore P. Saunders (*b.* 1957)

1 Lift high your hearts in blessing
    for all that God has done,
who sends, for our possessing,
    a Saviour and a Son!
On us and every nation
    how bright his mercies shine,
a sceptre of salvation,
    the Lord of David's line.

2 Prophetic tongues foretold him,
    his long-awaited hour,
and we by faith behold him
    who comes in love and power:
a Son who stooped to save us
    as God the Father willed;
the covenant he gave us
    is now at last fulfilled.

3 May we, his way preparing,
    his day of grace proclaim,
the word of life declaring
    through our Redeemer's Name!
Creation's new beginning
    has dawned upon our sky,
an end of strife and sinning,
    and peace with God Most High!

Timothy Dudley-Smith (b. 1926)

85

Morgenlied

87 87 D with refrain

Refrain

Lift the ban - ner, Church of E - rin, as we did in

Music: Frederick Charles Maker (1844–1927)

form - er days, Lord of all the na - tions name him,

Je - sus Christ: the one we praise.

1   Lift the banner, Church of Erin,
       as we did in former days,
    Lord of all the nations name him,
       Jesus Christ: the one we praise.
    Day by day may we God's children,
       many races, different tongues,
    live in hope, and by his Spirit,
       live in Christ who makes us one.

    *Lift the banner, Church of Erin,
       as we did in former days,
    Lord of all the nations name him,
       Jesus Christ: the one we praise.*

2   With Columba, Patrick, Brigid,
       faithful servants, saints of God.
    Give us grace to rise and follow
       where your saints and martyrs trod.
    Grace to serve, or leave, this island,
       in the steps of saints of old,
    serve the shepherd, who has led us,
       feed his sheep and guard his fold.

Verses 3 & 4 are found overleaf.

85 Words: © Paul Gilmore

Lift the ban- ner, Church of E - rin, as we did in

form - er days, Lord of all the na - tions name him,

Je - sus Christ: the one we praise.

3   Not long-past, the days of darkness,
         hardened hearts are with us still,
     saints today and modern martyrs,
         count the cost and do your will.
     Banner of the cross before us,
         giving all we have to give,
     trusting not in gold or idols,
         turn to Christ, we look and live.

4   Lord, renew the Church in Ireland,
         hard-pruned yes, yet strong of root,
     by your Holy Spirit make us,
         works of grace to bear you fruit.
     Ancient anthems, modern chorus,
         praising God the three in one,
     one our voice in many accents,
         glimpses of your kingdom come.

Paul Gilmore (b. 1968)
based on a hymn by
James Edward Archer (1860–1916)

Music: Tim Hughes (b. 1978)
arranged by Paul Leddington Wright (b. 1951)

here I am to say that you're my God; ____ and you're al-to-ge-ther
love - ly, al - to-ge-ther wor - thy, al - to-ge-ther won - der -
-ful to me. ____

And I'll ne - - - ver know how much it cost to see my sin up-on that cross. And I'll ne -

that cross. *So here I am to*

Words: Tim Hughes (*b.* 1978)

87

Bridegroom
Unison

87 87 6

1 Like the murmur of the dove's song,
   like the challenge of her flight,
   like the vigour of the wind's rush,
   like the new flame's eager might:
     come, Holy Spirit, come.

2 To the members of Christ's Body,
   to the branches of the Vine,
   to the Church in faith assembled,
   to her midst as gift and sign:
     come, Holy Spirit, come.

3 With the healing of division,
   with the ceaseless voice of prayer,
   with the power to love and witness,
   with the peace beyond compare:
     come, Holy Spirit, come.

Carl P. Daw, Jr (*b.* 1944)

Music: Peter Cutts (*b.* 1937)

88

Christir be our Light

Unison

1 Long - ing for light, we wait in dark-ness. Long-ing for truth, we turn to you. Make us your own, your ho - ly peo-ple, light for the world to see.

Refrain

Christ, be our light! Shine in our hearts.

Music: Bernadette Farrell (b. 1957)

Shine through the dark - - ness. Christ, be our light!

Shine in your church ga-thered to - day.

2   Longing for peace, our world is troubled.
    Longing for hope, many despair.
    Your word alone has pow'r to save us.
        Make us your living voice.

3   Longing for food, many are hungry.
    Longing for water, many still thirst.
    Make us your bread, broken for others,
        shared until all are fed.

4   Longing for shelter, many are homeless.
    Longing for warmth, many are cold.
    Make us your building, sheltering others,
        walls made of living stone.

5   Many the gifts, many the people,
    many the hearts that yearn to belong.
    Let us be servants to one another,
        making your kingdom come.

Bernadette Farrell (b. 1957)

89

Christ be our Light

1 This is the

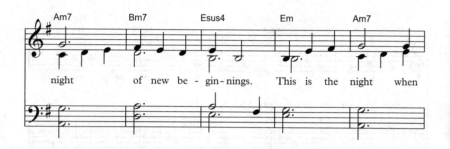

night of new be - gin - nings. This is the night when

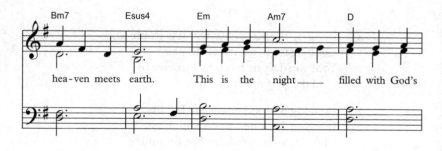

hea - ven meets earth. This is the night____ filled with God's

glo - ry, pro - mise of our new birth!_____

Please turn over for Refrain.

Music: Bernadette Farrell (b. 1957)

1   This is the night of new beginnings.
    This is the night when heaven meets earth.
    This is the night filled with God's glory,
        promise of our new birth!

Christ, be our light! Shine in our hearts.
    Shine through the darkness.
Christ, be our light!
    Shine in your church gathered today.

2   This is the night Christ our Redeemer
    rose from the grave triumphant and free,
    leaving the tomb of evil and darkness,
        empty for all to see.

3   Now will the fire kindled in darkness
    burn to dispel the shadows of night.
    Star of the morning, Jesus our Saviour,
        you are the world's true light!

4   Sing of the hope deeper than dying.
    Sing of the power stronger than death.
    Sing of the love endless as heaven,
        dawning throughout the earth.

5   Into this world morning is breaking.
    All of God's people, lift up your voice.
    Cry out with joy, tell out the story,
        all of the earth rejoice!

Bernadette Farrell (*b.* 1957)

89 Words: © 1990, 1991 Robert F O'Connor SJ and Wisconsin Province of The Society of Jesus. Published by OCP, 5536 NE Hassalo, Portland, OR 97213, USA. All rights reserved. Used with permission.

1 Lord, I come to you, ___ let my heart be
2 Lord, un-veil my eyes, ___ let me see you

changed, re - newed, ___ flow - ing from the
face to face, ___ the know-ledge of your

grace that I found ___ in you.
love as you live ___ in me.

And, Lord I've come to know
Lord, re - new my mind

Music: Geoff Bullock (b. 1956)

me, bring me near, draw me to your __ side; ___

___ and as I wait, I'll rise up like an

ea - - - gle, and I will soar with you; your Spi-rit leads me on

in the pow'r of your love. ___

Words: Geoff Bullock (b. 1956)

Music: Rick Founds (*b.* 1954)

You came from hea - ven to earth to show the way,

from the earth to the cross my debt to pay,

from the cross to the grave, from the grave to the sky:

Lord, I lift your name on high.

Words: Rick Founds (b. 1954)

92

She moved through the fair

LM

Unison

Lord__ make__ us ser - vants of__ your peace;

where_ there__ is hate,__ may we__ sow love;

where there__ is hurt,__ may we__ for give;

where__ there__ is strife, may_ we__ make one.

92 Arrangement: © Jacqueline Mullen

1   Lord, make us servants of your peace:
    where there is hate, may we sow love;
    where there is hurt, may we forgive;
    where there is strife, may we make one.

2   Where all is doubt, may we sow faith;
    where all is gloom, may we sow hope;
    where all is night, may we sow light;
    where all is tears, may we sow joy.

3   Jesus, our Lord, may we not seek
    to be consoled, but to console,
    nor look to understanding hearts,
    but look for hearts to understand.

4   May we not look for love's return,
    but seek to love unselfishly,
    for in our giving we receive,
    and in forgiving are forgiven.

5   Dying, we live, and are reborn
    through death's dark night to endless day;
    Lord, make us servants of your peace
    to wake at last in heaven's light.

James Quinn, SJ (1919–2010)
from a prayer attributed to
St Francis of Assisi (1182–1226)

These words may be sung to the tune FOLKSONG, *CH5* no. 399,
by adding a slur to the first notes of bars 2 and 6.

Music: Irish traditional melody
    arranged by Jacqueline Mullen (*b.* 1961)

93

Archer

11 10 11 10

Alternative tune: 133, EPIPHANY

Music: Malcolm Archer (*b.* 1952)
adapted from the anthem *Brightest and Best* by Julie Bell (*b.* 1979)

1   Lord, we have come at your own invitation,
        chosen by you, to be counted your friends;
    yours is the strength that sustains dedication,
        ours a commitment we know never ends.

2   Here, at your table, confirm our intention,
        ever to cherish the gifts you provide;
    teach us to serve, without pride or pretension,
        led by your Spirit, defender and guide.

3   When, at your table, each time of returning,
        vows are renewed and our courage restored:
    may we increasingly glory in learning ⌣
        all that it means to accept you as Lord.

4   So, in the world, where each duty assigned us
        gives us the chance to create or destroy,
    help us to make those decisions that bind us,
        Lord, to yourself, in obedience and joy.

                          Fred Pratt Green (1903–2000)

94

Christ arose

65 64 with refrain

Refrain

Up from the grave he a-rose,_____ with a migh-ty tri-umph o'er his

foes;_____ he a-rose a vic-tor from the dark do-main, and he

Music: Robert Lowry (1826–1899)

lives for ev - er with his saints to reign: He a - rose! _____

He a - rose! _____ Hal - le - lu - jah! Christ a - rose!

1 Low in the grave he lay,
   Jesus, my Saviour,
   waiting the coming day,
   Jesus, my Lord:

   Up from the grave he arose,
   with a mighty triumph o'er his foes;
   he arose a victor from the dark domain,
   and he lives for ever with his saints to reign:
   He arose! He arose!
   Hallellujah! Christ arose!

2 Vainly they watch his bed,
   Jesus, my Saviour;
   vainly they seal the dead,
   Jesus, my Lord:

3 Death cannot keep his prey,
   Jesus, my Saviour;
   he tore the bars away,
   Jesus, my Lord:

Robert Lowry (1826–1899)

95

Mayenziwe

Mayenziwe 'ntando yakho.
Mayenziwe 'ntando yakho.
Mayenziwe 'ntando yakho.
Mayenziwe 'ntando yakho.
Mayenziwe 'ntando yakho.

Your will be done on earth, O Lord.
Your will be done on earth, O Lord.
Your will be done on earth, O Lord.
Your will be done on earth, O Lord.
Your will be done on earth, O Lord.

Xhosa (South African) text,
from *The Lord's Prayer*

Music: South African traditional,
as taught by George Mxadana and transcribed in 1988 by John L. Bell.

Music: Anonymous
      arranged by Jacqueline Mullen (b. 1961)

tor - rents,   and   on - ly   eight were   saved.
rain - bow,   re - mem - ber   God   is   love.

1   Mister Noah built an ark,
    the people thought it such a lark.
       Mister Noah pleaded so,
          but into the ark they would not go.

    Down came the rain in torrents (splish, splash),
    down came the rain in torrents (splish, splash),
    down came the rain in torrents,
    and only eight were saved.

2   The animals went in two by two,
    elephant, giraffe and kangaroo.
       All were safely stowed away
          on that great and awful day.

    Down came the rain in torrents (splish, splash),
    down came the rain in torrents (splish, splash),
    down came the rain in torrents,
    and only eight were saved.

    Whenever you see a rainbow,
    whenever you see a rainbow,
    whenever you see a rainbow,
       remember God is love.

                                        Anonymous

97

Morning glory

7777

Music: Barry Rose (*b.* 1934)

1   Morning glory, starlit sky,
      leaves in springtime, swallows' flight,
    autumn gales, tremendous seas,
      sounds and scents of summer night;

2   Soaring music, towering words,
      art's perfection, scholar's truth,
    joy supreme of human love,
      memory's treasure, grace of youth;

3   Open, Lord, are these, thy gifts,
      gifts of love to mind and sense;
    hidden is love's agony,
      love's endeavour, love's expense.

4   Love that gives, gives evermore,
      gives with zeal, with eager hands,
    spares not, keeps not, all outpours,
      ventures all, its all expends.

5   Drained is love in making full;
      bound in setting others free;
    poor in making many rich;
      weak in giving power to be.

6   Therefore he who thee reveals
      hangs, O Father, on that tree ‿
    helpless; and the nails and thorns ‿
      tells of what thy love must be.

7   Thou art God, no monarch thou,
      throned in easy state to reign;
    thou art God, whose arms of love ‿
      aching, spent, the world sustain.

William Hubert Vanstone (1923–1999)

98

My God is so big, so strong and so migh-ty, there's no-thing that he can-not do. ___ My God is so big, so strong and so migh-ty, there's no-thing that he can-not do. ___

1 The ri - vers are his, the
2 He's called you to live for

Music: Anonymous

arranged by Jacqueline Mullen (*b.* 1961)

moun - tains are his, the stars are his hand - i - work
him ev - ery day, in all that you say and you

too. _____ My God is so big, so strong and so
do. _____

migh - ty, there's no - thing that he can - not do. _____

Words: Anonymous

1 My heart is filled with thank-ful-ness to him who bore my pain; who plumbed the depths of my dis-grace and gave me life a-gain; who crushed my curse of sin-ful-ness and clothed me in his light, and

Music: Stuart Townend (b. 1963) and Keith Getty (b. 1974)

wrote his law of right-eous-ness with power up-on my heart.

1   My heart is filled with thankfulness
        to him who bore my pain;
    who plumbed the depths of my disgrace
        and gave me life again;
    who crushed my curse of sinfulness,
        and clothed me in his light,
    and wrote his law of righteousness
        with power upon my heart.

2   My heart is filled with thankfulness
        to him who walks beside;
    who floods my weaknesses with strength
        and causes fear to fly;
    whose every promise is enough
        for every step I take;
    sustaining me with arms of love
        and crowning me with grace.

3   My heart is filled with thankfulness
        to him who reigns above;
    whose wisdom is my perfect peace,
        whose every thought is love.
    For every day I have on earth
        is given by the King.
    So I will give my life, my all,
        to love and follow him.

Stuart Townend (*b.* 1963)
and Keith Getty (*b.* 1974)

100

Solid Rock

LM with refrain

On Christ, the so - lid rock, I stand— all o - ther ground is

sink - ing sand, all o - ther ground is sink - ing sand.

Music: William Batchelder Bradbury (1816–1868)

1 My hope is built on nothing less
than Jesus' blood and righteousness;
   no merit of my own I claim,
   but wholly trust in Jesus' name.

   On Christ, the solid rock, I stand –
   all other ground is sinking sand,
   all other ground is sinking sand.

2 When weary in this earthly race,
I rest on his unchanging grace;
   in every wild and stormy gale
   my anchor holds and will not fail.

3 His vow, his covenant and blood
are my defence against the flood;
   when earthly hopes are swept away
   he will uphold me on that day.

4 When the last trumpet's voice shall sound,
O may I then in him be found!
   clothed in his righteousness alone,
   faultless to stand before his throne.

Edward Mote (1797–1874)

101

Gordon

Music: Adoniram J. Gordon (1836–1895), altd.

1   My Jesus, I love thee, I know thou art mine;
for thee all the pleasures of sin I resign;
    my gracious Redeemer, my Saviour art thou,
    if ever I loved thee, my Jesus, 'tis now.

2   I love thee because thou hast first lovèd me,
and purchased my pardon on Calvary's tree;
    I love thee for wearing the thorns on thy brow,
    if ever I loved thee, my Jesus, 'tis now.

3   I'll love thee in life, I will love thee in death,
and praise thee as long as thou lendest me breath;
    and say, when the death-dew lies cold on my brow,
    if ever I loved thee, my Jesus, 'tis now.

4   In mansions of glory and endless delight,
I'll ever adore thee in heaven so bright;
    I'll sing with the glittering crown on my brow,
    if ever I loved thee, my Jesus, 'tis now.

William R. Featherstone (1846–1873)

Music: Darlene Zschech (b. 1965)

Shout to the Lord all the earth, let us sing, pow-er and ma-
I sing for joy at the work of your hands. For - ev - er I'll love

- jes-ty, praise to the King. Moun-tains bow down and the seas
you, for-ev - er I'll stand. No - thing com-pares to the pro-

1st time

will roar at the sound of your name.

2nd time

- mise I have in you.

Words: Darlene Zschech (*b.* 1965)

103

How can I keep from singing   87 87 with refrain

Refrain

Music: Robert Lowry (1826–1899)

1 My life flows on in endless song
    above earth's lamentation:
I hear the real, though far-off hymn
    that hails a new creation.

No storm can shake my inmost calm
    while to that rock I'm clinging;
since Love is Lord of heaven and earth,
    how can I keep from singing?

2 Through all the tumult and the strife
    I hear that music ringing;
it finds an echo in my soul;
    how can I keep from singing?

3 What though my joys and comforts die,
    the Lord my Saviour liveth!
What though the darkness round me close,
    songs in the night he giveth.

4 The peace of Christ makes fresh my heart,
    a fountain ever springing.
All things are mine since I am his!
    How can I keep from singing?

Anonymous, first published New York, 1868

104

Junkanoo

Briskly

Now go in peace, now go in love, from the Fa-ther a-
-bove. Je - sus Christ the Son stay with you till the
day is done. Ho - ly Spi - rit en - cir - cle you
in all you think and do. Once a -
-gain God's bless - ing be with you. A - men.

This song may be sung as a round, the voices entering where indicated.

Music: Caribbean folk melody
  arranged by Michael Mair (b. 1942)

Now go in peace, now go in love,
from the Father above.
Jesus Christ the Son
stay with you till the day is done.
Holy Spirit encircle you
in all you think and do.
Once again God's blessing
be with you. Amen.

Michael Mair (b. 1942)

104 Words and Music: © Church of Scotland Panel on Worship

105

Music: John Carl Ylvisaker (*b.* 1937)
arranged by Julie Bell (*b.* 1979)

Refrain

Words: John Carl Ylvisaker (b. 1937)

106

Amazing Grace CM

For another arrangement of this tune see *CH5* no.642.

Music: Popular variant of early North American folk melody,
   possibly of Scottish origin
   arranged by Derek Verso (*b.* 1955)

1   Now through the grace of God we claim
        this life to be his own,
     baptized with water in the name
        of Father, Spirit, Son.

2   For Jesus Christ the crucified,
        who broke the power of sin,
     now lives to plead for those baptized
        in unity with him.

3   So let us act upon his word,
        rejoicing in our faith,
     until we rise with Christ our Lord
        and triumph over death!

                        Michael Perry (1942–1996)

107

Music: Stuart Townend (b. 1963) and Keith Getty (b. 1974)

out   to   those   in   dark - ness.

2 Our call to war, to love the captive soul
       but to rage against the captor;
   and with the sword that makes the wounded whole,
       we will fight with faith and valour.
   When faced with trials on every side
       we know the outcome is secure,
   and Christ will have the prize for which he died,
       an inheritance of nations.

3 Come see the cross, where love and mercy meet,
       as the Son of God is stricken;
   then see his foes lie crushed beneath his feet,
       for the Conqueror has risen!
   And as the stone is rolled away,
       and Christ emerges from the grave,
   this victory march continues till the day
       every eye and heart shall see him.

4 So Spirit, come, put strength in every stride,
       give grace for every hurdle,
   that we may run with faith to win the prize
       of a servant good and faithful.
   As saints of old still line the way,
       retelling triumphs of his grace,
   we hear their calls, and hunger for the day
       when with Christ we stand in glory.

Stuart Townend (b. 1963)
and Keith Getty (b. 1974)

107 Words and Music: © 2005 Thankyou Music. Administered by Capitol CMG Publishing, excl. UK & Europe, administered by
Integrity Music, part of the David C Cook family, <songs@integritymusic.com>

108

Plaisir d'amour

Music: Jean-Paul-Égide Martini (1741–1816)
harmonised by Jacqueline Mullen (b. 1961)

1   O God of Faith
      give me your Spirit and grace
  and guide me through all my days till ‿
      I see your face.

2   O God of Hope
      give light in dark times and strife,
  be with me now and for ever
      beyond this life.

3   O God of Love
      forgive the things I do wrong,
  rejoice in all that is perfect,
      keep me from harm.

4   O Father, Son
      and Holy Spirit divine,
  confirm within me your promise,
      new life is mine!

Jonathan Barry (b. 1947)

109

Resignation

1   O God, you are my God alone,
        whom eagerly I seek,
    though longing fills my soul with thirst
        and leaves my body weak.
    Just as a dry and barren land
        awaits a freshening shower,
    I long within your house to see
        your glory and your power.

2   Your faithful love surpasses life,
        evoking all my praise;
    through every day, to bless your name,
        my hands in joy I'll raise.
    My deepest needs you satisfy
        as with a sumptuous feast;
    so, on my lips and in my heart,
        your praise has never ceased.

3   Throughout the night I lie in bed
        and call you, Lord, to mind;
    in darkest hours I meditate
        how God, my strength, is kind.
    Beneath the shadow of your wing,
        I live and feel secure;
    and daily, as I follow close,
        your right hand keeps me sure.

John L. Bell (b. 1949)
based on Psalm 63:1-8

Music: American folk melody
    arranged by John L. Bell (b. 1949)

110

Music: Bernadette Farrell (b. 1957)

1   O God, you search me and you know me.
      All my thoughts lie open to your gaze.
    When I walk or lie down you are before me:
      ever the maker and keeper of my days.

2   You know my resting and my rising.
      You discern my purpose from afar,
    and with love everlasting you besiege me:
      in every moment of life or death, you are.

3   Before a word is on my tongue, Lord,
      you have known its meaning through and through.
    You are with me beyond my understanding:
      God of my present, my past and future, too.

4   Although your Spirit is upon me,
      still I search for shelter from your light.
    There is nowhere on earth I can escape you:
      even the darkness is radiant in your sight.

5   For you created me and shaped me,
      gave me life within my mother's womb.
    For the wonder of who I am, I praise you:
      safe in your hands, all creation is made new.

Bernadette Farrell (*b.* 1957)
based on Psalm 139

111

Donard

SM

Alternative tune: FRANCONIA, *CH5* no.630

Music: Peter Thompson (*b.* 1979)

1   O Lord, you knelt to wash ‿
      your first disciples' feet
before you faced the cross, and showed ‿
      your way of love complete.

2   They thought, 'How can the Christ,
      whose power and gifts we crave,
stoop down with towel and basin here,
      the posture of a slave?'

3   As then you came to serve ‿
      the twelve you called your friends,
so now you come to us in love
      that neither fades nor ends.

4   Lord Jesus, help us learn ‿
      what you would teach us still;
to serve in love, and share your joy
      in God your Father's will.

Basil Bridge (*b.* 1927)

112

Baldersdale   LM

Alternative tune: BRESLAU, *CH5* no. 599

Music: David Barton (*b.* 1981)

1   O merciful Creator, hear;
to us in pity bow thine ear:
   accept the tearful prayer we raise
   in this our fast of forty days.

2   Each heart is manifest to thee;
thou knowest our infirmity:
   repentant now we seek thy face;
   impart to us thy pardoning grace.

3   Our sins are manifold and sore,
but spare thou them who sin deplore;
   and for thine own name's sake make whole
   the fainting and the weary soul.

4   Grant us to mortify each sense
by means of outward abstinence,
   that so from every stain of sin
   the soul may keep her fast within.

5   Blest Three in One, and One in Three,
almighty God, we pray to thee,
   that thou wouldst now vouchsafe to bless
   our fast with fruits of righteousness.

Audi benigne conditor, 9th century or earlier
Compilers of *Hymns Ancient & Modern,* 1861
based on translation of John Mason Neale (1818–1866)

113

The power of the Cross

1 Oh, to see the dawn of the dark-est day:
tried by sin-ful men, torn and beat-en, then

Christ on the road to Cal-va-ry;
nailed to a cross of

Refrain

wood._____ This, the power_____ of the cross:_____

—— Christ be-came_____ sin for us;_____
(after v. 4) Son of God,_____ slain for us;_____

Music: Keith Getty (b. 1974) and Stuart Townend (b. 1963)

2   Oh, to see the pain written on your face,
     bearing the awesome weight of sin;
     every bitter thought, every evil deed,
        crowning your blood-stained brow.

3   Now the daylight flees, now the ground beneath
     quakes as its maker bows his head,
     curtain torn in two, dead are raised to life;
        'Finished!' the victory cry.

4   Oh, to see my name written in the wounds,
     for through your suffering I am free;
     death is crushed to death, life is mine to live;
        won through your selfless love.

This the power of the cross;
Son of God, slain for us;
what a love! What a cost!
We stand forgiven at the cross.

Keith Getty (*b.* 1974)
and Stuart Townend (*b.* 1963)

113 Words and Music: © 2005 Thankyou Music. Administered by Capitol CMG Publishing, excl. UK & Europe, administered by
Integrity Music, part of the David C Cook family, <songs@integritymusic.com>

114

Stille Nacht

Irregular

Oí - che chiúin, oí - che Mhic Dé,____ Cách 'na suan,____
Oí - che chiúin, oí - che Mhic Dé,____ Aoirí ar dtús____
Oí - che chiúin, oí - che Mhic Dé,____ Mac Dé bhí,____

dís ar - aon,____ Dís is díl - se ag faire le spéis,____
chuala an scéal,____ 'Ail - i - liu - ia' ain - gil ag glaoch,____
gáire a bhéil,____ Tuar dá rá 's dá lán - chur i gcéill,____

Naí beag gnaoi - gheal cean - án tais caomh, Críost ina chod - ladh go
Can - tain Shuairc i ngar is i gcéin, Críost ár Slán - ai - theoir
Ann gur thá - inig tráth chinn a tséinn, Críost a theacht ar an

séimh,____ Críost____ ina chod - ladh go séimh.____
féin,____ Críost____ ár Slán - i - theoir féin.____
saol,____ Críost____ a theacht ar an saol.____

114 Harmonisation: © APCK. *See after First Lines index for details.*

1 Oíche chiúin, oíche Mhic Dé,
cách 'na suan, dís araon,
dís is dílse ag faire le spéis,
naí beag gnaoi-gheal, ceananntais caomh;
Críost ina chodladh go séimh,
Críost ina chodladh go séimh.

2 Oíche chiúin, oíche Mhic Dé,
aoirí ar dtús chuala an scéal,
'Aililiuia' aingil ag glaoch,
cantain Shuairc i ngar is i gcéin;
Críost ár Slánaitheoir féin,
Críost ár Slánaitheoir féin.

3 Oíche chiúin, oíche Mhic Dé,
Mac Dé bhí, gáire a bhéil,
tuar dá rá 's dá lán-chur i gcéill,
ann gur tháinig tráth chinn a tséin,
Críost a theacht ar an saol,
Críost a theacht ar an saol.

Based on *Stille Nacht! Heilige Nacht!*
Joseph Mohr (1792–1848)
Irish version by Douglas Hyde
(Dubhghlas de hÍde) (1860–1949)

Music: Melody by Franz Xaver Gruber (1787–1863)
harmonised by Compilers of *Church Hymnal,* 1960

115

Baidín

Irregular

Unison

Capo 1

Music: Jacqueline Mullen (*b.* 1961)

1 One is the body and one is the head,
one is the Spirit by whom we are led;
one God and Father,
one faith and one call for all.

2 Christ who ascended to heaven above
is the same Jesus whose nature is love,
who once descended
to bring to this earth new birth.

3 Gifts have been given well-suited to each;
some to be prophets, to pastor or preach,
some, through the gospel,
to challenge, convert and teach.

4 Called to his service are women and men
so that his body might ever again
witness through worship,
through deed and through word to Christ our Lord.

John L. Bell (*b.* 1949)
based on Ephesians 4:11-16

116

Salley Gardens

Unison

76 76 D

Alternative tune: PASSION CHORALE, *CH5* no. 235

1 Our Father, we have wandered
     and hidden from your face,
in foolishness have squandered
     your legacy of grace.
But now, in exile dwelling,
     we rise with fear and shame,
as distant but compelling,
     we hear you call our name.

2 And now at length discerning
     the evil that we do,
behold us Lord, returning
     with hope and trust to you.
In haste you come to meet us
     and home rejoicing bring.
In gladness there to greet us
     with calf and robe and ring.

3 O Lord of all the living,
     both banished and restored,
compassionate, forgiving
     and ever caring Lord,
grant now that our transgressing,
     our faithlessness may cease.
Stretch out your hand in blessing
     in pardon and in peace.

Kevin Nichols (1926–2006)

Music: Irish folk melody, originally known as *The Maids of Mourne Shore*
arranged by Peter Thompson (b. 1979)

117

Music: Jo Hemming and Nigel Hemming

Coda

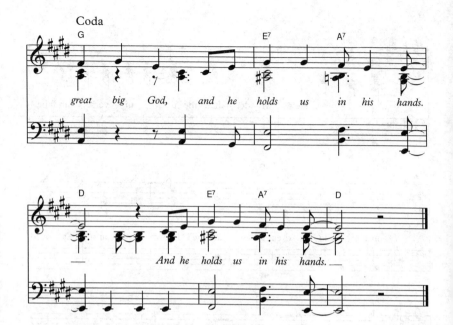

great big God, and he holds us in his hands.

And he holds us in his hands.

Our God is a great big God,
our God is a great big God,
our God is a great big God
and he holds us in his hands.
Our God is a great big God,
our God is a great big God,
our God is a great big God
and he holds us in his hands.

He's higher than a skyscraper
and he's deeper than a submarine.
He's wider than the universe
and beyond my wildest dreams.
And he's known me and he's loved me
since before the world began.
How wonderful to be a part
of God's amazing plan.

Our God is a great big God,
our God is a great big God,
our God is a great big God
and he holds us in his hands.
And he holds us in his hands.

Jo Hemming
and Nigel Hemming

118

Besançon carol

87 98 87

Peo - ple, look east and

Peo - ple, look

sing to - day:

east: _____

Peo - ple, look east:

Music: French traditional carol
harmonised by Martin Shaw (1875–1958)

1. People, look east. The time is near
   of the crowning of the year.
   Make your house fair as you are able,
   trim the hearth and set the table.
     People, look east and sing today:
     Love, the guest, is on the way.

2. Furrows, be glad. Though earth is bare,
   one more seed is planted there:
   Give up your strength the seed to nourish,
   that in course the flower may flourish.
     People, look east and sing today:
     Love, the rose, is on the way.

3. Birds, though ye long have ceased to build,
   guard the nest that must be filled.
   Even the hour when wings are frozen
   he for fledging time has chosen.
     People, look east and sing today:
     Love, the bird, is on the way.

4. Stars, keep the watch. When night is dim
   one more light the bowl shall brim,
   shining beyond the frosty weather,
   bright as sun and moon together.
     People, look east and sing today:
     Love, the star, is on the way.

5. Angels announce to man and beast
   him who cometh from the east.
   Set every peak and valley humming
   with the word, the Lord is coming.
     People, look east and sing today:
     Love, the Lord, is on the way.

Eleanor Farjeon (1881–1965)

118 Words: © Gervase Farjeon, from *The Children's Bells* (OUP) Used by permission of David Higham Associates Ltd, 5-8 Lower John Street, Golden Square, London W1R 4HA

119

Besançon carol   87 98 87

Music: French traditional carol
harmonised by Barry Rose (b. 1934)

1   People, look east to see at last
       hopes fulfilled from ages past:
       now in the promise of the morning,
       see, a brighter day is dawning,
         rich with the visions long foretold,
         prophets' dreams from days of old.

2   God reaffirms the gracious call:
       words of welcome meant for all;
       comfort enough for all our sorrows;
       justice shaping new tomorrows;
         mercy bears fruit in lives restored,
         freed to praise and serve the Lord.

3   Now, with the coming of the light,
       darkest fears are put to flight;
       see how the clouds of gloom are clearing,
       blown aside by hope's appearing.
         Jesus, the light of all our days,
         comes and sets our hearts ablaze.

4   Born of grace, a child so small
       hail the promised Lord of all!
       Nailed to a cross for our salvation,
       he shall rule God's new creation.
         Lift up your eyes, and look again:
         see, he comes in power to reign!

Martin Leckebusch (b. 1962)

120

Ellan Vannin

87 87 D

Music: Manx traditional folk melody
sometimes ascribed to J Townsend *(fl.* 1896)
arranged by Peter Thompson *(b.* 1979)

1 Praise the One who breaks the darkness
    with a liberating light.
  Praise the One who frees the prisoners
    turning blindness into sight.
  Praise the One who preached the gospel
    healing every dread disease,
  calming storms and feeding thousands
    with the very bread of peace.

2 Praise the One who blessed the children
    with a strong yet gentle word.
  Praise the One who drove out demons
    with a piercing two-edged sword.
  Praise the One who brings cool water
    to the desert's burning sand;
  from this well comes living water
    quenching thirst in every land.

3 Praise the one true love incarnate:
    Christ who suffered in our place.
  Jesus died and rose for many
    that we may know God by grace.
  Let us sing for joy and gladness
    seeing what our God has done.
  Praise the one redeeming glory,
    praise the One who makes us one.

Rusty Edwards *(b. 1955)*

121

Flexford

10 10 10 10 10 10

Alternative tune: 145 UNDE ET MEMORES

1   Pray for the Church, afflicted and oppressed,
        for all who suffer for the gospel's sake,
     that Christ may show us how to serve them best
        in that one Kingdom Satan cannot shake.
     But how much more than us they have to give,
     who by their dying show us how to live.

2   Pray for Christ's dissidents, who daily wait,
        as Jesus waited in the olive grove,
     the unjust trial, the pre-determined fate,
        the world's contempt for reconciling love.
     Shall all they won for us, at such a cost,
     be by our negligence or weakness lost?

3   Pray that if times of testing should lay bare
        what sort we are, who call ourselves his own,
     we may be counted worthy then to wear,
        with quiet fortitude, Christ's only crown:
     the crown that in his saints he wears again –
     the crown of thorns that signifies his reign.

                                    Fred Pratt Green (1903–2000)

Music: Hugh Benham (*b.* 1943)

122

Curfá

'Sé__ an Tiar - - na__ m'aoi - re, ní bheidh
aon__ ní de__ díth orm.

Fine   Véarsa

1 'Sé__ an Tiar - na__
2 Seo - lann sé mé ar rian - ta

m'aoi - re, ní bheidh aon__ ni de__ dhíth orm.
dí - rea - cha mar__ gheall ar a ai - nm. Fiú__ dá

Cuir - eann sé 'mo_____ luí__ mé i__
siúl fainn i ngleann an dor - cha - dais, níor__

Music: Fintan O'Carroll (1922–1981)

móin - - éar __ féir ____ ghlais; seo-lann sé ar imeall an __
bhaól liom an __ t-olc; ____ a - gus tú __ faram le do

uis - ce __ mé, mar a bhfaigh ____ im suaimhneas
shlat is do bhachall chun só - lás a thabhairt dom.

D.C.

Véarsa

3 Cói - ríonn tú bórd chun ____ béi - le __ dom i __
4 Lean - faidh cin - eál tas __ is __ fa - bhar mé gach __

bhfian - ai-se mo __ naimh - de; un-gann tú mo cheann le __
uile lá __ de mo shaol; ____ i ____ dteach an Tiar-na a __

D.C.

ho - - la; tá mo chu - pán ag cur thar maoil.
mhair- fidh _ mé go _ brách _____ na breithe.

'Sé an Tiarna m'aoire,
ní bheidh aon ní de díth orm.

1   'Sé an Tiarna m'aoire,
ní bheidh aon ní de díth orm.
Cuireann sé i mo luí mé i móinéar féar ghlais.
Seolann sé ar imeall an uisce mé,
mar a bhfaighim suaimhneas

2   Seolann sé mé ar rianta díreacha
mar gheall ar a ainm, fiú dá siúl
fainn i ngleann an dorchadais,
níor bhaol liom an t-olc;
agus tú farám le do shlat
is do bhachal chun sóláis a thabhairt dom.

3   Cóiríonn tú bord chun béile dom i bhfianaise mo naimhde
ungann tú mo cheann le hola;
tá mo chupán ag cur thar maoil;

4   Leanfaidh cineáltas is fabhar mé gach uile lá de mo shaol;
i dteach an Tiarna a mhairfidh mé go brách na breithe

Irish text
based on Psalm 23

123

Calypso carol   Irregular
Unison

1 See him ly - ing on a bed of straw: a draugh-ty sta - ble with an

o - pen door; _ Ma - ry cra - dl-ing the babe she bore, _ the

prince of glo - ry is his name. *O now car - ry me to*

Beth - le - hem _ to see the Lord _ of love a - gain: _

For another arrangement of this tune in a higher key (D) see *CH5* no. 689.

Music: Michael Perry (1942–1996)
        arranged by Christopher Tambling (b. 1964)

just as poor__ as was the sta - ble then, __ the

prince of glo - ry when he came.

sta - ble then, __ the prince of glo - ry when he came.

2   Star of silver, sweep across the skies,
show where Jesus in the manger lies;
shepherds, swiftly from your stupor rise
to see the saviour of the world!

3   Angels, sing again the song you sang,
sing the story of God's gracious plan;
sing that Bethl'em's little baby can
be the saviour of us all.

4   Mine are riches, from your poverty,
from your innocence, eternity;
mine, forgiveness by your death for me,
child of sorrow for my joy.

Michael Perry (1942–1996)

124

1   See the Lamb of God,
see the Lamb of God,
    nailed to a cross,
    suffering loss,
come see the Lamb of God.

2   Hear the Lamb of God,
hear the Lamb of God
    calling your name,
    taking your shame,
come hear the Lamb of God.

3   Love the Lamb of God,
love the Lamb of God.
    Give him your heart,
    he'll never depart,
come, love the Lamb of God.

4   See the Lamb of God,
see the Lamb of God,
    nailed to a cross,
    suffering loss,
come see the Lamb of God.

Edwin Brown

Music: Edwin Brown

125

1 See,_____ what a morn - ing, glo - - rious-ly
2 See_____ Ma - ry weep - ing, 'Where_____ is he
3 One_____ with the Fa - ther, An - - cient of

bright, with the dawn - - ing of hope in Je -
laid?' as in sor - - row she turns from the
Days, through the Spi - - rit who clothes faith with

-ru - - - - sa - lem; fold - - ed the
emp - - - ty tomb; hears_____ a voice
cer - - - tain - ty, ho - nour and

grave - clothes, tomb_____ filled with light, as the
speak - ing, call - - ing her name; it's the
bless - ing, glo - - - ry and praise to the

Music: Stuart Townend (b. 1963) and Keith Getty (b. 1974)

an - - gels an - nounce Christ is ri - - - - -
Mas - - ter, the Lord raised to life_____ a -
King crowned with power and au - tho - - - - ri -

-sen! See God's sal - -
-gain! The voice that
- ty! And we are

- va - - tion____ plan, wrought in love, borne in
spans the____ years, speak - ing life, stir - ing
raised with____ him, death is dead, love has

pain,____ paid in sac - - - - ri - fice,
hope,____ bring - ing peace_____ to us,
won,____ Christ has con - - - - quered;

ful - filled in Christ, the __ man, for he
will sound till he ap - pears, for he
and we shall reign with __ him, for he

lives; Christ is ri - sen from the dead. __

vv. 1,2

Last time

1   See, what a morning, gloriously bright
with the dawning of hope in Jerusalem;
folded the grave clothes, tomb filled with light,
as the angels announce Christ is risen!
   See God's salvation plan,
wrought in love, borne in pain, paid in sacrifice,
   fulfilled in Christ the man,
   for he lives; Christ is risen from the dead.

2   See Mary weeping, 'Where is he laid?'
as in sorrow she turns from the empty tomb;
hears a voice speaking, calling her name;
it's the Master, the Lord raised to life again!
   The voice that spans the years,
speaking life, stirring hope, bringing peace to us,
   will sound till he appears,
   for he lives; Christ is risen from the dead.

3   One with the Father, Ancient of Days,
through the Spirit who clothes faith with certainty,
honour and blessing, glory and praise
to the King crowned with power and authority!
   And we are raised with him,
death is dead, love has won, Christ has conquered;
   and we shall reign with him,
   for he lives; Christ is risen from the dead.

Stuart Townend (*b.* 1963)
and Keith Getty (*b.* 1974)

126

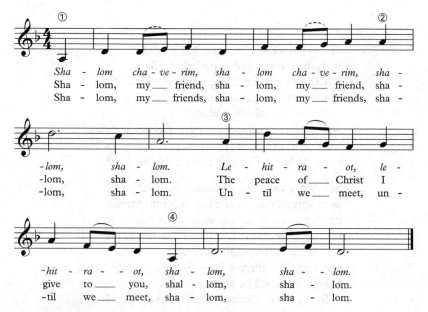

Sha - lom cha-ve-rim, sha - lom cha-ve-rim, sha -
Sha - lom, my __ friend, sha - lom, my __ friend, sha -
Sha - lom, my __ friends, sha - lom, my __ friends, sha -

-lom, sha - lom. Le - hit - ra - ot, le -
-lom, sha - lom. The peace of __ Christ I
-lom, sha - lom. Un - til we __ meet, un -

-hit - ra - - ot, sha - lom, sha - - lom.
give to __ you, shal - lom, sha - lom.
-til we __ meet, sha - lom, sha - lom.

This may be sung as a round, the voices entering where indicated,
using one or more verses in combination.

Shalom chaverim,
shalom chaverim,
shalom, shalom.
Lehitraot, lehitraot,
shalom, shalom.

Shalom, my friend,
shalom, my friend,
shalom, shalom.
The peace of Christ I give to you,
shalom, shalom.

Shalom, my friends,
shalom, my friends,
shalom, shalom.
Until we meet, until we meet,
shalom, shalom.

Hebrew blessing
tr. S. T. Kimbrough, Jr.

Music: Hebrew melody

127

1 Silent, surrendered, calm and still, open to the word of God. Heart humbled to his will, offered is the servant of God.

*2 Come Holy Spirit, bring us light, teach us, heal us give us life. Come, Lord, O let our hearts flow with love and all that is true.

v. 1 Pamela Hayes (1933–2001)
v. 2 Margaret Rizza (b. 1929)

Music: Margaret Rizza (b. 1929)

Verse 2 is intended for Pentecost. Either verse may be sung one or more times.

128

Music: Mark Johnson and Helen Johnson

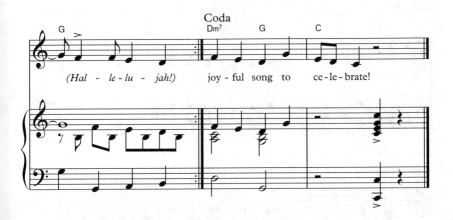

2 Clap your hands, clap your hands like this
clap your hands like this to celebrate!
Clap your hands, clap your hands like this
clap your hands like this to celebrate!

3 Jump up and down, up and down and around
up and down and around to celebrate!
Jump up and down, up and down and around
up and down and around to celebrate!

4 Dance to the beat, to the beat of the drum
to the beat of the drum to celebrate!
Dance to the beat, to the beat of the drum
to the beat of the drum to celebrate!

5 Wave your hands, wave your hands in the air
wave your hands in the air to celebrate!
Wave your hands, wave your hands in the air
wave your hands in the air to celebrate!

(Repeat verse 1 without refrain.)

Mark Johnson
and Helen Johnson

128 Words and Music: © 1995, 2008, Out of the Ark Limited, Unit F1 Kingsway Business Park, Oldfield Road, Hampton, Middlesex TW12 2HD

129

Scampston

Alternative tune: WOODLANDS, *CH5* no. 712

Music: Richard Shephard (*b.* 1949)

1   Sing, choirs of heaven! Let saints and angels sing.
    Around God's throne exult in harmony.
    Now Jesus Christ is risen from the grave.
    Salute your King in glorious symphony.

2   Sing, choirs of earth! Behold, your light has come!
    The glory of the Lord shines radiantly.
    Lift up your hearts, for Christ has conquered death.
    The night is past: the day of life is here.

3   Sing, church of God! Exult with joy outpoured.
    The gospel trumpets tell of victory won.
    Your Saviour lives: he's with you evermore.
    Let all God's people shout the long Amen.

based on *Exsultet jam angelica (The Easter Song of Praise)*

130

Trier

68 888 and Alleluias

Music: Melody by Johann Paul Schiebel (1764–1838)
as set to *Christus ist erstanden* in *Kölnisches Gesangbuch*, 1844
harmonised by Charles Wood (1866–1926)

1   Sing, God's Easter people, sing!
    For Jesus Christ of Nazareth
    who shared our life and tasted death
    has now been raised before the eyes
    of his astonished witnesses.
        Alleluia! Alleluia!

2   Sing, God's Easter people, sing!
    First Mary with sweet spices came,
    discovering the empty tomb.
    At once she ran, no time to lose,
    resolved to tell her friends the news.
        Alleluia! Alleluia!

3   Sing, God's Easter people, sing!
    Disciples John and Peter saw
    the Lord lay in the grave no more;
    and Thomas, later filled with doubt,
    found disbelief turned inside out.
        Alleluia! Alleluia!

4   Sing, God's Easter people, sing!
    Give thanks! The Lord Christ holds death's keys;
    stands in our midst, bestows his peace
    and sends us, strengthened, to enfold
    his scattered flock across the world.
        Alleluia! Alleluia!

                              David Mowbray (b. 1938)

131

Cliftonville

87 87 D

With movement

Alternative tune: ABBOT'S LEIGH, *CH5* no. 38

Music: John Crothers (*b.* 1948)

1   Sing of Andrew, John's disciple,
      led by faith through ways untrod,
till the Baptist cried at Jordan,
      'There behold the Lamb of God.'
Stirred by hearing this new teacher,
      Andrew, freed from doubt and fear,
ran to tell his brother Simon,
      'God's anointed One is here!'

2   Sing of Andrew, called by Jesus
      from the shores of Galilee,
leaving boats and nets and kindred,
      trusting in that 'Follow me.'
When a lad's small meal fed thousands,
      when inquiring Greeks found care,
when the Spirit came in blessing,
      Andrew faithfully was there.

3   Sing of Andrew, bold apostle,
      sent to make the gospel known,
faithful to his Lord's example,
      called to make a cross his own.
So may we who prize his memory
      honour Christ in our own day,
bearing witness to our neighbours,
      living what we sing and pray.

Carl P. Daw, Jr (*b.* 1944)

132

In the gloaming

87 87 D

Music: Annie Fortescue Harrison (1850–1944)
harmonised by Peter Thompson (b. 1979)

MARY

1 Sleep, my darling, I will watch you
    in the gentle candle glow.
Who are you? But while I wonder,
    angels, shepherds, wise men know.
Saviour, prophet, prince, Messiah?
    What will be, I do not know,
as I watch you, nurse you, love you,
    in the golden candle glow.

JOSEPH

2 Songs of angels, gifts from wise men,
    who is this, my Mary dear?
You have given us a son, who ‿
    draws the whole wide world so near.
On the hillside shepherds trembled
    when they heard the angel throng,
'Glory be to God the highest,
    peace on earth', the heaven song.

THE WORLD

3 O Messiah, Jesu, Saviour
    born for us in manger stall.
Bind us close that we may worship
    you as King and Lord of all.
When your star pierced through
        the darkness,
    wise men saw what lay below.
Pray that soon the world may glory
    in the golden gospel glow.

Jonathan Barry (*b.* 1947)

133

Epiphany

11 10 11 10

For this tune in a higher key (D) see *CH5* no. 190.

Music: Joseph Francis Thrupp (1827–1867)

1. Sons of the Holy One bright with his splendour,
       wakened to life at creation's new day,
   first to uplift in the joy of surrender
       spirits to worship and wills to obey.

2. Armies of Michael, a heavenly wonder,
       crashed to the onset with evil on high,
   till the proud angel, o'ercome by their thunder,
       dropped on his darkening wings from the sky.

3. Stars of the morn, for creation returning
       praise to the wisdom ordaining the whole,
   hushed their glad songs, in amazement discerning
       God's very likeness in man's living soul.

4. Sentries of Paradise, knew ye no sorrow,
       guarding the way with a flame of the sword?
   Visioned ye not on a glorious morrow
       man by a tree to his Eden restored?

5. Gabriel came with his high salutation,
       burning with ardour and eager in flight.
   'Ave Maria!' The dawn of salvation
       rose at its music and banished our night.

6. See, then, my soul, on a stairway all golden,
       angels ascending, descending again!
   Sion is here, if our eyes were not holden,
       praise would not fail for their service to men.

7. Praise God for Michael, in strife our defender,
       praise him for Raphael, our healer and guide,
   praise him for guardians, watchful and tender,
       true to their charges in need at their side.

8. Laud to thee, Father of spirits supernal!
       we with the angels adore thee, O Son!
   Comforter, holy, proceeding, eternal,
       in thee be glory to God, Three in One.

Francis Arthur Judd (1878–1939)

134

Music: Keith Getty (*b.* 1974) and Stuart Townend (*b.* 1963)

Words: Keith Getty (b. 1974) and Stuart Townend (b. 1963)

135

Spirit of God within me

76 86 86 86

Spi - rit of God with - in me,

pos - sess my hu - man frame; fan the dull em - bers

of my heart stir up the liv - ing flame.

Strive till that im - age Ad - am lost, new min - ted and re -

- stored _____ in shin - ing splen - dour bright - ly bears the

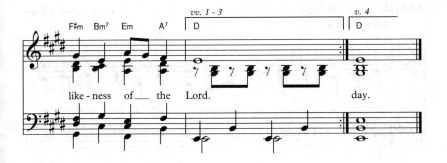

2   Spirit of truth within me,
        possess my thought and mind;
    lighten anew the inward eye
        by Satan rendered blind;
    shine on the words that wisdom speaks
        and grant me power to see
    the truth made known to all in Christ,
        and in that truth be free.

3   Spirit of love within me,
        possess my hands and heart;
    break through the bonds of self-concern
        that seeks to stand apart:
    grant me the love that suffers long,
        that hopes, believes and bears,
    the love fulfilled in sacrifice,
        that cares as Jesus cares.

4   Spirit of life within me,
        possess this life of mine;
    come as the wind of heaven's breath,
        come as the fire divine!
    Spirit of Christ, the living Lord,
        reign in this house of clay,
    till from its dust with Christ I rise
        to everlasting day.

Timothy Dudley-Smith (b. 1926)

Music: Michael Baughen (b. 1930)
      arranged by David Wilson (b. 1940)

136

Blow the wind southerly

13 10 13 10 with refrain

Refrain *Unison*

Spi-rit of ho-li-ness, wis-dom and faith-ful-ness, wind of the
Lord, blow-ing strong-ly and free: strength of our serv-ing and
joy of our wor-ship-ping – Spi-rit of God, bring your full-ness to
me!

Music: English traditional melody
arranged by John Barnard (b. 1948)

Spirit of holiness, wisdom and faithfulness,
wind of the Lord, blowing strongly and free:
strength of our serving and joy of our worshipping –
Spirit of God, bring your fullness to me!

1 You came to interpret and teach us effectively
   all that the Saviour has spoken and done;
   to glorify Jesus is all your activity –
   promise and gift of the Father and Son:

2 You came with your gifts to supply all our poverty,
   pouring your love on the church in her need;
   you came with your fruit for our growth to maturity,
   richly refreshing the souls that you feed:

3 You came to the world in its pride and futility,
   warning of dangers, directing us home;
   now with us and in us, we welcome your company;
   Spirit of Christ, in his name you have come:

Christopher Idle (*b.* 1938)

THANKS & PRAISE

137

FIRST TUNE

Hendon

77 77 extended

Music: Henri Abraham César Malan (1787–1864)
arranged by Peter Thompson (b. 1979)

137.i Arrangement: © Peter Thompson

137

SECOND TUNE

Mo ghile mear   77 77

1   Spirit of the Lord, come down,
      spreading your protective wing
over all that you have made,
      over every living thing.

2   Come in storm-wind, cleansing fire,
      sweeping through a world unclean;
come in every gentle breeze:
      breath of God, unheard, unseen.

3   Holy Spirit, blessèd Light,
      guide and strengthen mind and will;
comfort every grieving heart,
      and our inmost being fill.

4   Through the Father and the Son,
      by whose blood our life was bought,
fill our empty hands with gifts:
      come with grace unearned, unsought.

Community of Stanbrook Abbey

Music: 18th-century Irish traditional melody
    arranged by Peter Thompson (b. 1979)

137.ii Arrangement: © Peter Thompson
137 Words: © Stanbrook Abbey, Wass, York YO61 4AY UK

138

Some or all of the optional verses, for one or more cantors, may be added once the ostinato has been sung at least twice.

(Continues on opposite page.)

pray, watch and pray!

pray not to give way to temp-ta - tion.

but the flesh is weak.

-main here with me, stay a-wake and pray.

if it is pos-si-ble, let this cup pass me by.

drink-ing it, your will be done.

the Lord is com-ing!

pray, watch and pray.

Words: Taizé Community
based on Matthew 26:36-42

Music: Jacques Berthier (1923–1994)

139

Music: Keith Getty (b. 1974) and Kristyn Getty (b. 1980)

ser-vant to all. ___ If you wan-na be great, if you

wan-na be tall, you must be ___ a ser-vant to all.

Stop and think, don't be so fast.
If you wanna be first, you must be last.
It's upside down and hard to do,
but you should put others first before you.

If you wanna be great,
if you wanna be tall,
you must be a servant to all.

If you wanna be great,
if you wanna be tall,
you must be a servant to all.

Keith Getty (*b.* 1974)
and Kristyn Getty (*b.* 1980)

140

Divine Mysteries   66 66 88 6 extended

Music: Francis Stanfield (1835–1914)

1   Sweet Sacrament divine,
    the Lamb upon the throne
    reveals in bread and wine,
    the life that is his own.
    Jesu, to thee our voice we raise
    in songs of love and heartfelt praise:
    sweet Sacrament divine,
    sweet Sacrament divine.

2   Sweet Sacrament of peace,
    dear home for every heart,
    where restless yearnings cease
    and sorrows all depart;
    there in thine ear all trustfully
    we tell our tale of misery:
    sweet Sacrament of peace,
    sweet Sacrament of peace.

3   Sweet Sacrament of rest,
    ark from the ocean's roar,
    within thy shelter blest
    soon may we reach the shore;
    save us, for still the tempest raves,
    save, lest we sink beneath the waves:
    sweet Sacrament of rest,
    sweet Sacrament of rest.

4   Sweet Sacrament divine,
    earth's light and jubilee,
    in thy far depths doth shine
    the Godhead's majesty;
    sweet light, so shine on us, we pray
    that earthly joys may fade away:
    sweet Sacrament divine,
    sweet Sacrament divine.

        Francis Stanfield (1835–1914), altd.

141

1 Tag-ai-mis le ché-ile os— comhair an Rí, siúil, siúil i
2 Is guí- mis le ché-ile dár— nAth - air thuas,
3 Tá Di- a— beo— ag-us gránn sé thú,

so - las Dé.— Agus can-ai-mis le ché-ile le grá 'nár— gcroí,
Go gcu-ire sé a chab - hair chug-ainn an - uas,
Níl aon— áit— don——— ghru - aim níos mó,

siúil, siúil i so - las— Dé. Siúil,———

siúil i so - las Dé, siúil,——— siúil i so - las Dé,

siúil, _____ siúil i so-las Dé, siúil-ai-mis i so - las Dé.

1   Tagaimis le chéile os comhair an Rí,
siúil, siúil i solas Dé.
Agus canaimis le chéile le grá 'nár gcroí
siúil, siúil i solas Dé

Siúil, siúil i solas Dé
siúil, siúil i solas Dé
siúil, siúil i solas Dé
siúilaimis i solas Dé

2   Is guímis le chéile dár nAthair thuas,
siúil, siúil i solas Dé.
Go gcuire sé a chabhair chugainn anuas.
siúil, siúil i solas Dé.

3   Ta Dia beo agus gránn sé thú
siúil, siúil i solas Dé.
Níl aon áit don ghruaim níos mó
siúil, siúil i solas Dé

Irish version of *Walk in the light*
by Damian Lundy (1944–1997)

Music: Damian Lundy (1944–1997)
    arranged by Donald Davison (1937–2013)

142

Take, O take me as I am;

sum-mon out what I shall be;

set your seal up-on my heart and live in me.

Since there are no accidentals, this setting may be read a
semitone higher, in the key of D, if desired.

Take, O take me as I am;
summon out what I shall be;
set your seal upon my heart
and live in me.

John L. Bell (*b.* 1949)

Music: John L. Bell (*b.* 1949)

Music: Graham Kendrick (b. 1950) and Steve Thompson

teach me to trust in the word of your pro - mise, teach me to hope
in the day of your com - ing, teach me to dance to the

to verses *last time*

beat of your heart.

Verse

1 You wrote the rhy - thm of life, cre - a - ted hea - ven and earth,
2 Let all my move-ments ex-press a heart that loves to say 'yes',

in you is joy with-out mea - sure. So, like a
a will that leaps to o - bey____ you. Let all my

child in your sight, I dance to see your de-light, for I was made for your
en-er-gy blaze to see the joy in your face; let my whole be - ing

plea - - - - sure, plea - - - - sure.
praise____ you, praise____ you.

Words: Graham Kendrick (b. 1950)
and Steve Thompson

144

Laredo

12 10 12 11 Irregular

Music: American cowboy melody, derived from Irish folk melody,
collected by John A. Lomax

1   The Church is wherever God's people are praising,
      knowing they're wanted and loved by their Lord;
the Church is wherever Christ's followers are trying
      to live and to share out the good news of God.

2   The Church is wherever God's people are loving,
      where all are forgiven and start once again,
where all are accepted, whatever their background,
      whatever their past and whatever their pain.

3   The Church is wherever God's people are seeking
      to reach out and touch folk wherever they are –
conveying the Gospel, its joy and its comfort,
      to challenge, refresh, and excite and inspire.

4   The Church is wherever God's people are praising,
      knowing we're wanted and loved by our Lord;
the Church is where we as Christ's followers are trying
      to live and to share out the good news of God.

Carol Rose Ikeler (1920–2013)

145

Unde et memores 10 10 10 10 10 10

For this tune in a lower key (D) see *CH5* no. 400.

Music: William Henry Monk (1823–1889)

1   The hour has come, foretold since time began,
when on that cross there hangs the Son of Man,
and through what pain his prayer is heard in heaven
that those who drove the nails might be forgiven.
   The dying thief is promised 'You shall be
this very day in Paradise with me'.

2   He charges Mary, and that well-loved one,
be now his mother, and be now her son.
The world's true light in darkness dies alone,
and asks why God should so forsake his own;
   while, as the powers of evil do their worst,
the living water, too, becomes 'I thirst'.

3   The Prince of life, his earthly purpose done,
cries 'Finished' now, a world's salvation won,
and as the gate of heaven open stands
commends his spirit to his Father's hands:
   soon from his three-day grave to rise again,
to rise in glory, and in glory reign.

Timothy Dudley-Smith (b. 1926)
based on the seven words from the cross

146

Paderborn

10 10 11 11

Music: German folk melody included in *Gesangbuch,* Paderborn, 1765
arranged by Sydney Hugo Nicholson (1875–1947)

1   The kingdom of God is justice and joy,
    for Jesus restores what sin would destroy;
        God's power and glory in Jesus we know,
        and here and hereafter the kingdom shall grow.

2   The kingdom of God is mercy and grace,
    the lepers are cleansed, the sinners find place,
        the outcast are welcomed God's banquet to share,
        and hope is awakened in place of despair.

3   The kingdom of God is challenge and choice,
    believe the good news, repent and rejoice!
        His love for us sinners brought Christ to his cross,
        our crisis of judgement for gain or for loss.

4   God's kingdom is come, the gift and the goal,
    in Jesus begun, in heaven made whole;
        the heirs of the kingdom shall answer his call,
        and all things cry glory to God all in all!

Bryn Rees (1911–1983)

147

1 The Lord's my shep - herd, I'll not want. He makes me lie in pas - tures green. He leads me by the still, still wa - ters, his good-ness re-stores my soul.

Descant

I will trust, I will trust in you.

Refrain

And I will trust in you a - lone, and I will

Music: Stuart Townend (*b.* 1963)

I will trust, I will trust in you. End - less mer - cy

trust in you a - lone, for your end - less mer - cy

fol - lows me, good - ness will lead me home.

fol - lows me, your good - ness will lead me home.

2   He guides my ways in righteousness,
      and he anoints my head with oil,
      and my cup, it overflows with joy,
        I feast on his pure delights.

3   And though I walk the darkest path,
      I will not fear the evil one,
      for you are with me, and your rod and staff
        are the comfort I need to know.

Stuart Townend (b. 1963)
based on Psalm 23

147 Words and Music: © 1996 Thankyou Music. Administered by Capitol CMG Publishing, excl. UK & Europe, administered by Integrity Music, part of the David C Cook family, <songs@integritymusic.com>

148

Afton Water

76 76 with refrain

Unison

Oh, the food comes from the ba - ker, the drink comes from the vine, __ the words come from the Sa - viour, 'I will meet you in bread and wine.'

Music: Scottish traditional melody, collected 1792
arranged by Peter Thompson (*b.* 1979)

1   The time was early evening,
        the place a room upstairs;
     the guests were the disciples,
        together saying prayers.

     Oh, the food comes from the baker,
        the drink comes from the vine,
     the words come from the Saviour,
        'I will meet you in bread and wine.'

2   The company of Jesus
        had met to share a meal,
     but he, who made them welcome,
        had much more to reveal.

3   'The bread and body broken,
        the wine and blood outpoured,
     the cross and kitchen table
        are one by my sign and word.'

4   On both sides of the table,
        on both sides of the grave,
     the Lord joins those who love him
        to serve them and to save.

5   Lord Jesus, now among us,
        confirm our faith's intent,
     as, with your words and actions,
        we unite in this sacrament.

     Verse 3 should be sung solo.

John L. Bell (*b.* 1949)
and Graham Maule (*b.* 1958)

149

The Virgin Mary

Irregular

The Vir-gin Ma - ry had a ba-by boy, _ the

Vir-gin Ma - ry had a ba-by boy, _ the Vir-gin Ma - ry had a

Music: West Indian traditional
arranged by John Barnard (b. 1948)

ba-by __ boy, __ and they say that his name was Je — - sus. __

The Refrain is found overleaf.

1   The virgin Mary had a baby boy,
     the virgin Mary had a baby boy,
     the virgin Mary had a baby boy,
         and they say that his name was Jesus.

     He come from the glory,
         he come from the glorious kingdom.
     He come from the glory,
         he come from the glorious kingdom:
     O yes, believer! O yes, believer!
     He come from the glory,
         he come from the glorious kingdom!

2   The angels sang when the baby born,
     the angels sang when the baby born,
     the angels sang when the baby born,
         and proclaim him the Saviour Jesus.

3   The wise men went where the baby born,
     the wise men went where the baby born,
     the wise men went where the baby born,
         and they say that his name was Jesus.

                              West Indian carol

Verse *Unison*

1 There is a high - er throne than all this
2 And there we'll find our home, our life be -

world has known, where faith - ful ones from ev - ery tongue
-fore the throne; we'll ho - nour him in per - fect song

will one day come. Be - fore the
where we be - long. He'll wipe each

Son we'll stand, made fault - less through the Lamb; be -
tear - stained eye, as thirst and hun - ger die; the

Music: **Keith Getty** (b. 1974) **and Kristyn Getty** (b. 1980)
arranged by Julie Bell (b. 1979)

-liev - ing hearts find pro - mised grace: salva-tion
Lamb be-comes our Shep - herd King: we'll reign with

comes.
him.

Hear hea-ven's voi-ces sing, their thun-derous

an - them rings through em - erald courts and sap - phire skies,

their prai - ses rise. All glo - ry, wis - dom, power,

1   There is a higher throne
    than all this world has known,
    where faithful ones from every tongue
        will one day come.
    Before the Son we'll stand,
    made faultless through the Lamb;
    believing hearts find promised grace:
        salvation comes.

    Hear heaven's voices sing,
    their thunderous anthem rings
    through emerald courts and sapphire skies,
        their praises rise.
    All glory, wisdom, power,
    strength, thanks and honour are
    to God, our King who reigns on high
        for evermore.

2   And there we'll find our home,
    our life before the throne;
    we'll honour him in perfect song
        where we belong.
    He'll wipe each tear-stained eye,
    as thirst and hunger die;
    the Lamb becomes our Shepherd King:
        we'll reign with him.

Keith Getty (*b.* 1974)
and Kristyn Getty (*b.* 1980)

151

The truth from above

LM

Music: English traditional melody
Harmony adapted from his *Fantasia on Christmas Carols*
by Ralph Vaughan Williams (1872–1958)

1   This is the truth sent from above
the truth of God, the God of love;
     therefore don't turn me from your door
     but hearken all both rich and poor.

2   The first thing that I do relate
is that God did man create
     the next thing which to you I'll tell
     woman was made with man to dwell.

3   And after that, 'twas God's own choice
to place them both in Paradise,
     there to remain of evil free
     except they ate of such a tree.

4   But they did eat, which was a sin,
and so their ruin did begin,
     ruined themselves, both you and me,
     and all of their posterity.

5   Thus we were heirs to endless woes
till God and Lord did interpose
     and so a promise soon did run
     that he would redeem us by his Son.

6   And at that season of the year
our blessed Redeemer did appear
     he here did live and here did preach
     and many thousands he did teach.

7   Thus he in love to us behaved
to show us how we must be saved
     and if you want to know the way
     be pleased to hear what he did say.

English folk carol
collected from Shropshire by Cecil Sharp (1859–1924), altd.

152

Refrain

This lit‑tle light of mine, ___ I'm gon‑na let it shine; this lit‑tle light of mine, ___ I'm gon‑na let it shine; ___ this lit‑tle light of mine, I'm gon‑na let it shine; ___ let it shine, let it shine, ___ let it shine.

To verses

Music: American popular melody, sometimes attributed to
Harry Dixon Loes (1895–1965)
arranged by Peter Thompson (b. 1979)

shine my light both far and near, __ I'm gon - na
Fri - day he told me just to watch and pray, __

shine my light both bright and clear, __ where
Sa - tur - day he told me just what to say, __ on

there's a dark cor - ner in this land __ I'm gon - na
Sun - day he gave me the power di - vine __ to

let my lit - tle light shine.
let my lit - tle light shine.

This little light of mine, I'm gonna let it shine;
this little light of mine, I'm gonna let it shine;
this little light of mine, I'm gonna let it shine;
let it shine, let it shine, let it shine.

1 The light that shines is the light of love,
lights the darkness from above,
it shines on me and it shines on you,
and shows what the power of love can do.
I'm gonna shine my light both far and near,
I'm gonna shine my light both bright and clear,
where there's a dark corner in this land
I'm gonna let my little light shine.

2 On Monday he gave me the gift of love,
Tuesday peace came from above,
on Wednesday he told me to have more faith,
on Thursday he gave me a little more grace,
Friday he told me just to watch and pray,
Saturday he told me just what to say,
on Sunday he gave me the power divine
to let my little light shine.

possibly based on a song by
Harry Dixon Loes (1895–1965)

153

Thuma mina

Music: South African traditional hymn
adapted by Anders Nyberg (b. 1955)

Cantor: *Thuma mina.*
All: *Thuma mina, thuma mina,*
thuma mina, Somandla.

1 *Cantor:* Send me Lord.
All: Send me, Jesus, send me, Jesus,
send me, Jesus, send me, Lord.

2 *Cantor:* Lead me Lord.
All: Lead me, Jesus, lead me, Jesus,
lead me, Jesus, lead me, Lord.

3 *Cantor:* Fill me Lord.
All: Fill me, Jesus, fill me, Jesus,
fill me, Jesus, fill me, Lord.

Cantor: *Thuma mina.*
All: *Thuma mina, thuma mina,*
thuma mina, Somandla.

Xhosa original
adapt. Anders Nyberg (*b.* 1955)

153 Words and Music: From *Freedom Is Coming*, 1990. © 1990 Wild Goose Publications, Iona Community, Glasgow G2 3DH
Scotland. All rights reserved. Used by permission.

154

My Desire

1 To be in your pre - sence,
2 To rest in your pre - sence,

to sit at your feet,
not rush-ing a - way;

where your love sur-
to che - rish each

-rounds me,
mo - ment,

and makes me com - plete.
here I would stay.

Refrain

This is my de - sire, O__ Lord, this is my de - sire.

This is my de - sire, O__ Lord, this is my de-

-sire.

Words: Noël Richards (*b.* 1955)

Music: Noël Richards (*b.* 1955)
    arranged by Derek Verso (*b.* 1955)

155

Music: **Maggi Dawn** (*b.* 1959)

Wash me clean in that cool river;
wash my soul in the pure water.
Wash me clean in that cool river;
Lord, make me new.

Maggi Dawn (b. 1959)

156

Rachel

DCM

This tune was written for the words 'How sweet the name of Jesus sounds', *CH5* no. 92.
Alternative tune: WILTSHIRE, *CH5* no. 372

1 We bring you, Lord, our prayer and praise
   that every child of earth
  should live and grow in freedom's ways,
   in dignity and worth.

2 We praise for such a task begun
   to serve each other's need,
  for every cause of justice won,
   for every fetter freed.

3 Our prayers are for a world in pain
   where force and fear prevail,
  the plough becomes the sword again,
   and hope and harvests fail.

4 Alike our prayer and praise express
   the wants of humankind,
  that those in bondage and distress
   their larger freedoms find.

5 So may we still maintain the fight
   till earth's oppressions cease
  before the universal right
   to liberty and peace.

6 In Christ we learn to love and care
   and spread his truth abroad;
  and in his name we lift our prayer:
   'Your kingdom come, O Lord.'

Timothy Dudley-Smith (b. 1926)

Two verses of the text are sung to each repetition of the tune.

Music: Christopher Alan Bowater (b. 1947)
  arranged by Noël Tredinnick (b. 1949)

157

Nettleton

87 87 D

For another arrangement of this tune (suitable for unison singing)
in a lower key (C) see no. 28.

Music: American folk melody, in John Wyeth's
Repository of Sacred Music, Part Second, 1813
arranged by Peter Thompson (*b.* 1979)

1   We pray thee, heavenly Father,
      to hear us in thy love,
and pour upon thy children
      thy blessing from above;
that so in love abiding,
      from all defilement free,
we may in pureness offer
      our eucharist to thee.

2   All that we have we offer,
      for it is all thine own,
all gifts, by thine appointment,
      in bread and cup are shown;
one thing alone we bring not,
      the wilfulness of sin,
and all we bring is nothing
      save that which is within.

3   Within the pure oblation,
      beneath the outward sign,
by that his operation,
      the Holy Ghost divine,
lies hid the sacred body,
      lies hid the precious blood,
once slain, now ever glorious,
      of Christ our Lord and God.

4   Wherefore, though all unworthy
      to offer sacrifice,
we pray that this our duty
      be pleasing in thine eyes;
for praise, and thanks and worship,
      for mercy and for aid,
the Church's great thanksgiving
      for Jesus Christ is made.

Vincent Stuckey Stratton Coles (1845–1929), altd.

158

Isle of Innisfree
Unison

II IO II IO D

158 Music: © Hal Leonard Corporation, PO Box 13819, Milwaukee, WI 53213, USA. Permission applied for.

Alternative tune: LONDONDERRY AIR, *CH5* no. 303

1   We shall go out with hope of resurrection,
    we shall go out, from strength to strength go on;
    we shall go out and tell our stories boldly,
        tales of a love that will not let us go.
    We'll sing our songs of wrongs that can be righted,
    we'll dream our dream of hurts that can be healed,
    we'll weave a cloth of all the world united
        within the vision of a Christ who sets us free.

2   We'll give a voice to those who have not spoken,
    we'll find the words for those whose lips are sealed,
    we'll make the tunes for those who sing no longer,
        vibrating love alive in every heart.
    We'll share our joy with those who are still weeping,
    chant hymns of strength for hearts that break in grief,
    we'll leap and dance the resurrection story
        including all within the circles of our love.

                                    June Boyce-Tillman (*b.* 1943)

Music: Richard Farrelly (1916–1990)
    arranged by Jacqueline Mullen (*b.* 1961)

159

1 When it's all been said and done, — there is
just one thing that mat - - - - - ters; did I
do my _ best to live _ for truth, did I live my life _ for you?

to next verse

Music: Jim Cowan (b. 1952)

2 When it's all been said and done,
all my treasures will mean nothing;
only what I've done for love's reward,
will stand the test of time.

3 Lord, your mercy is so great,
that you look beyond our weakness;
and find purest gold in miry clay,
making sinners into saints.

4 I will always sing your praise;
here on earth and ever after;
for you've shown me heaven's
my true home,
when it's all been said and done,
you're my life when life is gone.

Jim Cowan (b. 1952)

160

St Louis

86 86 D

This tune was written for the words 'O little town of Bethlehem', *CH5* no. 174.
Alternative tune: KINGSFOLD, *CH5* no. 576

Music: Lewis H. Redner (1831–1908)

1   When Joseph went to bed one night,
      he lay awhile and wept ‿
that his young love, his own Mary
      betrayed him, so he thought;
but as the peace of sleep crept o'er,
      he gave himself to dream;
an angel of the Lord appeared
      and said what it did mean.

2   'God has come down from heav'n in truth
      and stands upon the earth;
he enters into all our lives
      turns sadness into mirth.
It is his Son who is our Lord,
      his name Emmanuel;
your baby Jesus is the one
      the prophets did foretell.'

3   Now is the time we should rejoice –
      the world's a better place,
the love of God shines bright and clear
      for all the human race.
The darkness of our lives outside
      reminds us of our sin;
when we accept the dear Christ-child
      the light shines from within.

Jonathan Barry (b. 1947)

161

Smithford Street   86 86 D

Unison

Alternative tune: KINGSFOLD, *CH*5 no. 576

Music: David Barton (b. 1983)

1   When pain and terror strike by chance,
       with causes unexplained,
when God seems absent or asleep,
       and evil unrestrained,
we crave an all-controlling force,
       ready to rule and warn,
but find, far-shadowed by a cross,
       a child in weakness born.

2   We marvel at God's nakedness
       and sense the play of chance
in Herod's anger, Peter's growth,
       and Pilate's troubled glance.
Our Saviour's tempted, tested way
       never was cut and dried,
but costly, risking life and love,
       betrayed and crucified.

3   How deep the Wisdom of our God,
       how weak, but truly wise,
to risk, to sacrifice, to die,
       and from the grave arise,
to shred the shroud of death and fate,
       freeing our hearts for good.
We breathe the ample air of hope
       and take our chance with God.

4   Since Wisdom took its chance on earth,
       to show God's living way,
we'll trust that fear and force will fail,
       and Wisdom win the day.
Then, come, dear Christ, and hold us fast
       when faith and hope are torn,
and bring us, in your loving arms,
       to resurrection morn.

Brian Wren (b. 1936)

162

It is well with my soul

Irregular

Music: Philipp Paul Bliss (1838–1876)

1 When peace, like a river, attendeth my way,
       when sorrows, like sea-billows, roll,
   whatever my lot, thou hast taught me to say,
       it is well, it is well with my soul.

   It is well with my soul,
   it is well, it is well with my soul.

2 Though Satan should buffet, though trials should come,
       let this blest assurance control,
   that Christ has regarded my helpless estate,
       and has shed his own blood for my soul.

3 My sin – O the bliss of this glorious thought! –
       my sin, not in part, but the whole,
   is nailed to his cross, and I bear it no more:
       praise the Lord, praise the Lord, O my soul!

4 For me be it Christ, be it Christ hence to live;
       if Jordan above me shall roll,
   no pang shall be mine, for in death as in life
       thou wilt whisper thy peace to my soul.

5 But, Lord, 'tis for thee, for thy coming, we wait;
       the sky, not the grave, is our goal;
   O trump of the angel! O voice of the Lord –
       blessèd hope, blessèd rest of my soul!

Horatio Gates Spafford (1828–1888)

163

Widford

76 76 77 76

Alternative tune: KELVINGROVE, *CH5* no. 605

Music: John Barnard (b. 1948)

1 When you prayed beneath the trees,
  it was for me, O Lord;
when you cried upon your knees,
  how could it be, O Lord?
When in blood and sweat and tears
you dismissed your final fears,
when you faced the soldiers' spears,
  you stood for me, O Lord.

2 When their triumph looked complete,
  it was for me, O Lord,
when it seemed like your defeat,
  they could not see, O Lord!
When you faced the mob alone
you were silent as a stone,
and a tree became your throne;
  you came for me, O Lord.

3 When you stumbled up the road,
  you walked for me, O Lord,
when you took your deadly load,
  that heavy tree, O Lord;
when they lifted you on high,
and they nailed you up to die,
and when darkness filled the sky,
  it was for me, O Lord.

4 When you spoke with kingly power,
  it was for me, O Lord,
in that dread and destined hour,
  you made me free, O Lord;
earth and heaven heard you shout,
death and hell were put to rout,
for the grave could not hold out;
  you are for me, O Lord.

Christopher Idle (b. 1938)

164

Armageddon (Wenn ich Ihn nur habe)   65 65 triple

Music: Melody possibly by Luise Reichardt
   adapted by John Goss (1800–1880)

1 Who is on the Lord's side?
　Who will serve the King?
Who will be his helpers
　other lives to bring?
Who will leave the world's side?
　Who will face the foe?
Who is on the Lord's side?
　Who for him will go?
By thy call of mercy,
　by thy grace divine,
we are on the Lord's side;
　Saviour, we are thine.

2 Jesus, thou hast bought us,
　not with gold or gem,
but with thine own life-blood,
　for thy diadem.
With thy blessing filling
　each who comes to thee,
thou hast made us willing,
　thou has made us free.
By thy great redemption,
　by thy grace divine,
we are on the Lord's side;
　Saviour, we are thine.

3 Not for weight of glory,
　not for crown and palm,
enter we the army,
　raise the warrior-psalm;
but for love that claimeth
　lives for whom he died:
he whom Jesus nameth
　must be on his side.
By thy love constraining,
　by thy grace divine,
we are on the Lord's side;
　Saviour, we are thine.

4 Fierce may be the conflict,
　strong may be the foe;
but the King's own army
　none can overthrow.
Round his standard ranging,
　victory is secure;
for his truth unchanging
　makes the triumph sure.
Joyfully enlisting,
　by thy grace divine,
we are on the Lord's side;
　Saviour, we are thine.

5 Chosen to be soldiers
　in an alien land,
chosen, called, and faithful,
　for our captain's band,
in the service royal
　let us not grow cold;
let us be right loyal,
　noble, true, and bold.
Master, thou wilt keep us,
　by thy grace divine,
always on the Lord's side;
　Saviour, always thine.

Frances Ridley Havergal (1836–1879)

164

SECOND TUNE

Rachie

65 65 triple

By thy call of mer - cy, by thy grace a -lone,

By thy call of mer - cy, by thy grace a - lone, ___

Music: Caradog Roberts (1878–1935)

1   Who is on the Lord's side?
      Who will serve the King?
   Who will be his helpers
      other lives to bring?
   Who will leave the world's side?
      Who will face the foe?
   Who is on the Lord's side?
      Who for him will go?
   By thy call of mercy,
      by thy grace divine,
   we are on the Lord's side;
      Saviour, we are thine.

2   Jesus, thou hast bought us,
      not with gold or gem,
   but with thine own life-blood,
      for thy diadem.
   With thy blessing filling
      each who comes to thee,
   thou hast made us willing,
      thou has made us free.
   By thy great redemption,
      by thy grace divine,
   we are on the Lord's side;
      Saviour, we are thine.

3   Not for weight of glory,
      not for crown and palm,
   enter we the army,
      raise the warrior-psalm;
   but for love that claimeth
      lives for whom he died:
   he whom Jesus nameth
      must be on his side.
   By thy love constraining,
      by thy grace divine,
   we are on the Lord's side;
      Saviour, we are thine.

4   Fierce may be the conflict,
      strong may be the foe;
   but the King's own army
      none can overthrow.
   Round his standard ranging,
      victory is secure;
   for his truth unchanging
      makes the triumph sure.
   Joyfully enlisting,
      by thy grace divine,
   we are on the Lord's side;
      Saviour, we are thine.

5   Chosen to be soldiers
      in an alien land,
   chosen, called, and faithful,
      for our captain's band,
   in the service royal
      let us not grow cold;
   let us be right loyal,
      noble, true, and bold.
   Master, thou wilt keep us,
      by thy grace divine,
   always on the Lord's side;
      Saviour, always thine.

Frances Ridley Havergal (1836–1879)

165

Mwamba

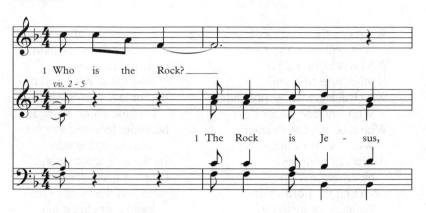

1 Who is the Rock?

vv. 2 - 5

1 The Rock is Je - sus,

Who is the Rock?

the Rock. The Rock is Je - sus, the Rock.

Music: East African Chant
transcribed by J. Nathan Corbett (*b.* 1950)
arranged by Geoff Weaver (*b.* 1943)

1   Who is the Rock?
    the Rock is Jesus the Rock.
    Who is the Rock?
    the Rock is Jesus the Rock.

2   He blesses us:
    the Rock is Jesus the Rock.
    He blesses us:
    the Rock is Jesus the Rock.

3   He heals from sin:
    the Rock is Jesus the Rock.
    He heals from sin:
    the Rock is Jesus the Rock.

4   The Rock protects:
    the Rock is Jesus the Rock.
    The Rock protects:
    the Rock is Jesus the Rock.

5   Who is the Rock?
    the Rock is Jesus the Rock.
    Who is the Rock?
    the Rock is Jesus the Rock.

J. Nathan Corbett (b. 1950)

166

Scarlet ribbons
Unison

87 87 D

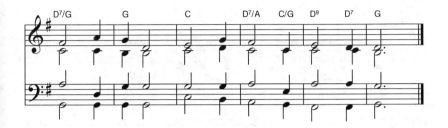

1 Who would think that what was needed
   to transform and save the earth
might not be a plan or army,
   proud in purpose, proved in worth?
Who would think, despite derision,
   that a child might lead the way?
God surprises earth with heaven,
   coming here on Christmas Day.

2 Shepherds watch and wise men wonder,
   monarchs scorn and angels sing;
such a place as none would reckon
   hosts a holy helpless thing;
stable beasts and by-passed strangers
   watch a baby laid in hay:
God surprises earth with heaven,
   coming here on Christmas Day.

3 Centuries of skill and science
   span the past from which we move,
yet experience questions whether,
   with such progress, we improve.
While the human lot we ponder,
   lest our hopes and humour fray,
God surprises earth with heaven,
   coming here on Christmas Day.

John L. Bell (*b.* 1949)
and Graham Maule (*b.* 1958)

The tune DRUMRAINEY (no. 9) was written for these words.

Music: Evelyn Danzig (1901–1996)
   arranged by John L. Bell (*b.* 1949)

167

With Christ in the vessel

With Je-sus in the boat we can smile at the storm, smile at the storm, smile at the storm. With Je-sus in the boat we can smile at the storm, as we go sail-ing home. *Sail - - ing, sail - ing home,*

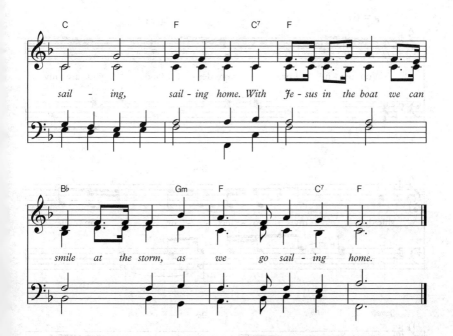

sail - ing, sail - ing home. With Je - sus in the boat we can

smile at the storm, as we go sail - ing home.

With Jesus in the boat
we can smile at the storm,
smile at the storm,
smile at the storm.
With Jesus in the boat
we can smile at the storm,
as we go sailing home.

Sailing, sailing home,
sailing, sailing home.
With Jesus in the boat
we can smile at the storm,
as we go sailing home.

Anonymous

Music: Anonymous
  arranged by Jacqueline Mullen (b. 1961)

Music: Doug Horley (b. 1953)

Lord, won-der-ful God, help me to trust you for ev - - er. I need not fear, 'cause you are near, I can lie down and sleep in peace.

Words: **Doug Horley** (*b.* 1953)

168 Words and Music: © 2003 Thankyou Music. Administered by Capitol CMG Publishing, excl. UK & Europe, administered by Integrity Music, part of the David C Cook family, <songs@integritymusic.com>

169

Was lebet, was schwebet   11 10 11 10

For this tune in a higher key (D) see *CH5* no. 196.

Music: Melody from *Rheinhardt MS,* 1754

1   Word of the Father, the life of creation,
        emptied of glory, among us you came;
     born as a servant, assuming our weakness,
        drank from the cup of our joy and our shame.

2   Each human child bears your image and likeness,
        yet all are heirs to the sins of our earth;
     once from death's flood you arose to redeem us,
        water and Spirit now seal our rebirth.

3   Searching, you found us before we could name you,
        loving, you suffered our pain and our loss;
     strengthen this child through the faith of your people,
        born in the glory which streams from the cross.

                          Colin Peter Thompson (b. 1945)

170

Hillbrow 87 87

Descant (v. 5)

5 Praise the ev- er- last - - - ing Fa - ther

and the Word, his — on - ly Son; praise the

Ho - ly Spi - rit, Tri - ni - ty in One.

Alternative tune: LAUS DEO (REDHEAD NO.46), *CH5* no. 316

Music: John Ewington (b. 1936)
descant Simon Lole (b. 1957)

1   Worship, glory, praise and honour
        to our God, high-throned above:
    we, with many generations,
        join to praise thy name of love.

2   Here by faith we mark our children
        with the cross of Christ our Lord,
    pray they may become Christ's soldiers
        and, with us, obey his word.

3   In the scriptures, by the Spirit,
        may we see the Saviour's face,
    hear his word and heed his calling,
        know his will and grow in grace.

4   Sanctify us by thy Spirit,
        Jesus, Lord, our corner-stone;
    make us each a holy temple
        built for God and God alone.

5   Praise the everlasting Father
        and the Word, his only Son;
    praise them through the Holy Spirit,
        perfect Trinity in One.

Maurice Arthur Ponsonby Wood (1916–2007)

171

Music: Dennis L Jernigan (b. 1959)

2 Taking my sin, my cross, my shame,
  rising again I bless your name,
   you are my all in all.
  When I fall down you pick me up,
  when I am dry you fill my cup,
   you are my all in all.

  Jesus, Lamb of God, worthy is your name.
  Jesus, Lamb of God, worthy is your name.

Dennis L Jernigan (b. 1959)

172

Music: J Larsson
arranged by Chris Mischief

can't stop God from lov - ing you, his love is new each

To next verse morn - - - ing. 2 You

Last time ev - - - er.

2   You can't stop ice from being cold,
          you can't stop fire from burning,
      or hold the tide that's going out,
          delay its sure returning,
      or halt the progress of the years,
          the flight of fame or fashion,
      you can't stop God from loving you,
          his nature is compassion.

3   You can't stop God from loving you
          though you may disobey him,
      you can't stop God from loving you,
          however you betray him;
      from love like this no power on earth
          the human heart can sever,
      you can't stop God from loving you,
          not God – not now, nor ever.

John Gowans (1934–2012)

173

Eagle's wings

(♩ = 84 - 96)

1 You who dwell in the shel-ter of the Lord, who a-
2 Snares of the fowl – er will nev-er cap-ture you, and
3 For to his an – gels he's giv-en a com-mand to

- bide in his sha-dow for life,
fa – mine will bring you no fear:
guard you in all of your ways;

say to the Lord, 'My re – fuge, my
un – der his wings your re – fuge, with
up – on their hands they will bear you up, lest you

Music: Michael Joncas (b. 1951)

rock   in whom   I   trust!'
faith - ful - ness_____   your   shield.
dash   your foot a - gainst a   stone.

Refrain

And he will raise you up on ea - gle's wings, bear you on the

breath of dawn, make you to shine_ like the sun, and

hold you in_ the_ palm of his hand.

Words: Michael Joncas (b. 1951)
based on Psalm 91 and Isaiah 40:31

174

Capel

CM

Music: English traditional melody
harmonised by Ralph Vaughan Williams (1872–1958)

1   Your words to me are life and health;
      put strength into my soul;
    enable, guide, and teach my heart
      to reach its perfect goal.

2   Your words to me are light and truth;
      from day to day I know ‿
    their wisdom, passing human thought,
      as in their truth I grow.

3   Your words to me are full of joy,
      of beauty, peace and grace;
    from them I learn your perfect will,
      through them I see your face.

4   Your words are perfected in one,
      yourself, the living Word;
    print your own image in my heart
      in clearest lines, my Lord.

George Currie Martin (1865–1937)

175

Lion of Judah

1 You're the Li - on of Ju - dah, the Lamb that was
2 There's a shield in our hand and a sword at our

slain, you as - cen - ded to hea - ven and e - ver - more will reign; at the
side, there's a fire in our spi - rit that can - not be de - nied; as the

end of the age when the earth you re - claim, you will ga - ther the
Fa - ther has told us: for these you have died, for the na - tions that

Music: Robin Mark (*b.* 1969)

as the King of all

kings and the Lord of all lords.'

The guitar chords are not always compatible with the four-part harmony.

Words: Robin Mark (*b.* 1969)

LITURGICAL SECTION

176

KYRIE ELEISON

Music: Peter Thompson (*b.* 1979)
Armagh Setting

Lord, have ___ mer - cy. Lord, have ___ mer - - cy.

Thi - arna, déan tró - cai - re. A Thi - arna, déan tró - cai - re.

Optional tone for sung petitions

Kyrie

Lord have mercy.
Lord have mercy.
Christ have mercy.
Christ have mercy.
Lord have mercy.
Lord have mercy.

A Thiarna, déan trócaire.
A Thiarna, déan trócaire.
A Chríost, déan trócaire.
A Chríost, déan trócaire.
A Thiarna, déan trócaire.
A Thiarna, déan trócaire

Holy Communion Two
Book of Common Prayer, 2004

176 Words: © 2004, RCB. *See after First Lines index for details.*

GLORIA IN EXCELSIS

Music: Peter Thompson (b. 1979)
Armagh Setting

Un poco meno mosso

mp

Lord Je-sus Christ, on-ly Son of the Fa - ther, Lord God, Lamb of

God, you take a - way the sin of the world: have mer - cy on

us; you are seat-ed at the right hand of the Fa - ther, re -

Je - sus Christ, with the Ho - - ly ___ Spi - rit, in the

glo - ry of God the Fa - ther. A - men! A - - men!

Glo - ry to God in the high - est, and peace to God's peo - ple on earth;

Gloria in excelsis

Glory to God in the highest,
and peace to God's people on earth.
Glory to God in the highest,
and peace to God's people on earth.

Lord God, heavenly King,
almighty God and Father,
we worship you, we give you thanks,
we praise you for your glory.

Glory to God in the highest,
and peace to God's people on earth.

Lord Jesus Christ, only Son of the Father,
Lord God, Lamb of God,
you take away the sin of the world:
have mercy on us;
you are seated at the right hand of the Father,
receive our prayer.

Glory to God in the highest,
and peace to God's people on earth.

For you alone are the Holy One,
you alone are the Lord,
you alone are the Most High,
Jesus Christ, with the Holy Spirit,
in the glory of God the Father. Amen! Amen!

Glory to God in the highest,
and peace to God's people on earth.

Holy Communion Two
Book of Common Prayer, 2004

178

GLORIA IN EXCELSIS

Gloria in excelsis

Glory to God in the highest,
and peace to God's people on earth.

Lord God, heaven|ly King,
almighty | God and Father,
we worship you, we | give you thanks,
we praise you | for your glory.

Lord Jesus Christ, only Son of | the Father,
Lord God, | Lamb of God,
you take away the sin of the world: ⌣
    have | mercy on us;
you are seated at the right hand of the Father, ⌣
    re|ceive our prayer.

For you alone are | the Holy One,
you alone | are the Lord,
you alone are the Most High, ⌣
    Jesus Christ, with the | Holy Spirit,
in the glory of God the Father. | Amen.

Holy Communion Two
Book of Common Prayer, 2004

Music: Peter Thompson (b. 1979)
   Armagh Setting

179

ALLELUIA

Al - le-lu - ia! Al - le-lu - ia! Al - le-lu - ia!

Chant for optional verses:

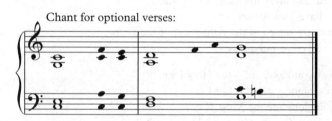

Alleluia

Alleluia! Alleluia! Alleluia!

Music: Peter Thompson (*b.* 1979)
Armagh Setting

180

GOSPEL GREETING

Gospel Greeting

Before the Gospel:
Glory to you, Lord Jesus Christ.

After the Gospel:
Praise to you, Lord Jesus Christ.

Holy Communion Two
Book of Common Prayer, 2004

Music: Peter Thompson (b. 1979)
Armagh Setting

181

SANCTUS AND BENEDICTUS

Music: Peter Thompson (b. 1979)
Armagh Setting

Words: Holy Communion Two
Book of Common Prayer, 2004

182

ACCLAMATION

Christ has died. Christ is ris - en.

Christ will come a - gain. Christ has died.

Christ is ris - en. Christ will come a - gain.

Words: Holy Communion Two
Book of Common Prayer, 2004

Music: Peter Thompson (b. 1979)
Armagh Setting

183

BLESSING AND HONOUR

Blessing and Honour

Blessing and honour and glory and power
are yours for ever and ever. Amen.

Holy Communion Two
Book of Common Prayer, 2004

Music: Peter Thompson (*b.* 1979)
Armagh Setting

184

GREAT AMEN

Great Amen

Amen. Amen.
Amen. Amen.
Amen. Amen.
Amen. Amen.

Music: Peter Thompson (*b.* 1979)
   Armagh Setting

185

AGNUS DEI

Lamb ___ of God, you ___ take ___ a - way the ___

A Uain _____ Dé, is ___ tú a ___ thó - gann ___

vv. 1, 2

sin ___ of the world, have mer - cy ___ on ___

pea - caí an domhain, déan tró - caire ___ or -

Music: Peter Thompson (*b.* 1979)
Armagh Setting

us.

- ainn

v. 3

sin____ of the world, grant us,

pea - caí an domhain, deo - - naigh

grant   us   your   peace.

dú - inn   sío - - - - cháin.

Agnus Dei

Lamb of God, you take away the sin of the world, have mercy on us.
Lamb of God, you take away the sin of the world, have mercy on us.
Lamb of God, you take away the sin of the world, grant us peace.

A Uain Dé, is tú a thógann peacaí an domhain, déan trócaire orainn.
A Uain Dé, is tú a thógann peacaí an domhain, déan trócaire orainn.
A Uain Dé, is tú a thógann peacaí an domhain, deonaigh dúinn síocháin.

Holy Communion Two
Book of Common Prayer, 2004

186

GLORIA IN EXCELSIS

Glo-ry to God in the high - est, and peace to God's peo-ple on earth. ___ Lord _ God, hea -ven - ly King, ___ al - -migh - ty God _ and Fa - ther, we wor - ship you, _ we give _ you thanks, we praise _ you for ___ your glo - ry.

Music: Alison Cadden (b. 1965)
St Columba Setting

Lord Je - sus Christ, on - ly Son of the Fa - ther, Lord God, __

Lamb __ of God, you take a - way __ the sin of the world: have

mer - cy on us; you __ are seat - ed at the right hand of the Fa - ther, re-

-ceive __ our prayer. __ For you a - lone are the Ho - ly One,

you a-lone are the Lord,___ you a-lone are the Most_ High,

Je - sus Christ, with the Ho - ly___ Spi - rit, in the

glo-ry of God the Fa - ther.___ A - - - - men.

Words: Holy Communion Two
Book of Common Prayer, 2004

187

Before Gospel

GOSPEL GREETING

Glo - ry to you, Lord Je - - sus___ Christ.

After Gospel

Praise to you, Lord Je - - sus___ Christ.

Gospel Greeting

Before the Gospel:
Glory to you, Lord Jesus Christ.

After the Gospel:
Praise to you, Lord Jesus Christ.

Holy Communion Two
Book of Common Prayer, 2004

Music: Alison Cadden (*b.* 1965)
St Columba Setting

187 Music: © A J Cadden
187 Words: © 2004, RCB. *See after First Lines index for details.*

188

SANCTUS AND BENEDICTUS

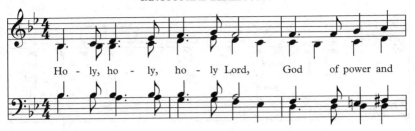

Ho - ly, ho - ly, ho - ly Lord, God of power and

might, heaven and earth are full of your glo - ry. Ho-

- san - na in the high - est! Blessed is he who comes in the

name of the Lord. Ho - san - na in the high - est!

Music: Alison Cadden (b. 1965)
  St Columba Setting

Words: Holy Communion Two
  Book of Common Prayer, 2004

189

THE LORD'S PRAYER

Our Fa - ther in hea - ven, hal - lowed be your name, _____ your king - dom come, your will be done, on earth _ as in hea - - - - ven. Give us to - day our dai - ly bread. For - give us our sins as we for - give

Music: Alison Cadden (b. 1965)
St Columba Setting

a - - gainst us.

those who sin a - - gainst us. Lead us

not in - to temp - ta - tion but de - li - ver us from

e - vil. For the king - dom, the power, and the glo - ry are yours

now and for ev - er. A - - men, A - - men.

Words: Holy Communion Two
Book of Common Prayer, 2004

190

AGNUS DEI

Je - - - sus, Lamb _ of

God, _ have mer-cy on us. _ Je - sus,

bear - er of _ our sins, _ have mer - cy on us. _

Je - sus, Re - deem - er of _ the world, _ grant _

190 Music: © A J Cadden

Agnus Dei

Jesus, Lamb of God, have mercy on us.
Jesus, bearer of our sins, have mercy on us.
Jesus, Redeemer of the world, grant us peace.

Holy Communion Two
Book of Common Prayer, 2004

Music: Alison Cadden (b. 1965)
St Columba Setting

191

Music: Dinah Reindorf (*b. c.* 1927)
　　arranged by Geoff Weaver (*b.* 1943)

1 Kyrie eleison. Kyrie eleison.
   Kyrie eleison. Kyrie eleison.

2 Christe eleison. Christe eleison.
   Christe eleison. Christe eleison.

3 Kyrie eleison. Kyrie eleison.
   Kyrie eleison. Kyrie eleison.

Liturgical text

The original setting consists of the Kyrie verse only.

192

1,3 Ky - ri - e   e - lei - son.   Ky - ri - e   e - lei - son.
2 Chri - ste   e - lei - son.   Chri - ste   e - lei - son.

Ky - ri - e   e - lei - son.
Chri - ste   e - lei - son.

1 Kyrie eleison.
   Kyrie eleison.
   Kyrie eleison.

2 Christe eleison
   Christe eleison
   Christe eleison.

3 Kyrie eleison.
   Kyrie eleison.
   Kyrie eleison.

Liturgical text

The original setting consists of the Kyrie verse only.

Music: Ukrainian traditional chant

193

Perry Street

Lord, have mer - cy. **Lord, have mer - cy.**

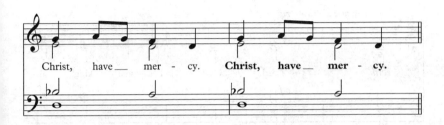

Christ, have mer - cy. **Christ, have mer - cy.**

Lord, have mer - cy **Lord, have mer - cy.**

This setting may be performed by a cantor (or choir) singing the first bar of each line, and the assembly singing the response.

1 Lord, have mercy.
Lord, have mercy.

2 Christ, have mercy.
Christ, have mercy.

3 Lord, have mercy.
Lord, have mercy.

Liturgical text

Music: Norman Warren (b. 1934)

194

Music: Fintan O'Carroll (1922–1981)

A little slower

Lord Je - sus Christ, on - ly __ Son of the

Fa - ther, Lord God, Lamb of __ God,

you take a - way the sin of the world: have mer - cy on

us; you are seat-ed at the right hand of the

glo - ry of God the___ Fa - ther.

A - - - - - men.

Words: Holy Communion Two
Book of Common Prayer, 2004

195

Music: Mike Anderson (b. 1955)

Verse

1 Lord God, hea-ven-ly King, _ peace you bring to

us; we wor-ship you, _ we give you thanks, _ we

sing our song _ of praise: _____

2 Jesus, Saviour of all,
   Lord God, Lamb of God,
   you take away our sins.
   Oh Lord, have mercy on us all.

3 At the Father's right hand,
   Lord receive our prayer,
   for you alone are the Holy One,
   and you alone are Lord.

4 Glory, Father and Son,
   glory, Holy Spirit,
   to you we raise our hands up high,
   we glorify your name:

Mike Anderson (b. 1955)

195 Words and Music: © Mike Anderson

196

Glo-ry to God, glo-ry to God, glo-ry in the high - est!
Son of the Fa - ther!
glo-ry to the Spi - rit!

Glo - ry to God, glo-ry to God, glo-ry in the high - est!
Son of the Fa - ther!
glo-ry to the Spi - rit!

To God be glo-ry for ev - er! *To God be glo-ry for ev - er!*

Al - le - lu - ia! A - men. *Al - le - lu - ia! A - men.*

Al - le - lu - ia! A - men. *Al - le - lu - ia! A - men.*

Al - le - lu - ia! A - men. *Al - le - lu - ia! A - men.*

Words: Peruvian liturgical text
collected by John Ballantine (b. 1945)

Music: Peruvian traditional chant

197

May be sung in unison, in harmony, or as a four-part round
(the voices entering where indicated).

Gloria, gloria in excelsis Deo!
Gloria, gloria, alleluia, alleluia.

Taizé Community

Music: Taizé Community
arranged by Julie Bell (b. 1979)

198

Curfá

Glóir__ do Dhia sna har - da   a - gus sío - cháin do

pho - bal Dé   ar chlár_____ an ta - laimh. __

Deireadh

Ái - - méan, ái - méan,__ ái - - - méan.

Music: Mark Duley

Véarsa

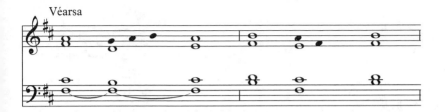

Glóir do Dhia sna harda
agus síocháin do phobal Dé ar chlár an talaimh.

A Thiarna Dia, a | Rí na bhflaitheas,
a Dhia uilechumhachtaigh | agus a Athair,
tugaimid adhradh agus | altú duit,
agus molaímid thú as ucht | do mhórghlóire.

A Thiarna Íosa Críost, a | Aonmhic an Athar,
A Thiarna Dia, a | Uain Dé,
tusa a thógann peacaí an domhain:
déan | trócaire orainn;
tá tú i do shuí ar dheis an Athar;
glac | lenár nguí.

Óir is tusa amháin an | Duine Naofa,
is tusa amháin | an Tiarna,
is tú amháin an tArd-Dia, |
a Íosa Críost, mar aon leis an Spiorad Naomh,
i nglóir Dé | an tAthair.

Áiméan.

Holy Communion Two
Book of Common Prayer, 2004

198 Words and Music: © 2014 Mamusa Editions

199

Music: Michael Joncas (b. 1951)

Hea-ven and earth are full _ of your glo - ry. Ho-san-na in the

high - est! Bless - ed is he, bless - ed is he who

Bless - - ed, blest is he who

comes in the name of the Lord Most High. Ho-san-na in the high-est,

Congregation

Ho-san-na in the high - est!

in __ the __ high - est! Ho-san-na in the high - est!

Words: Liturgical text, ELLC

200

Scarborough fair   Irregular

Unison

1   Holy, holy, holy Lord,
    God of endless power and might,
    the earth, the heavens are full of your love.
    Sing hosanna! Glory to God!

2   Blest is he, the one who is sent
    in the name of God the Most High.
    O holy, holy, holy our Lord!
    Sing hosanna! Glory to God!

Michael Forster (*b.* 1946)

Music: Variant of English traditional ballad melody
        arranged by Derek Verso (*b.* 1955)

201

Music: John Pantry (b. 1946)
    arranged by Jacqueline Mullen (b. 1961)

Words: Holy Communion Two
Book of Common Prayer, 2004

Music: based on Nikolai Andreyevich Rimsky-Korsakov (1844–1908)
Liturgy of St John Chrysostom, Op. 22 No. 7

Words: Liturgical text

203

Music: Joseph Lees (*fl.* 1911)

king - dom, ____ the power, and the glo - -

-ry, for ev - - - er and ev - - - er. ____

dim.
A - - - - men, ____ a - - - men.

dim.

Our Father, who art in heaven,
hallowèd be thy name,
thy kingdom come,
thy will be done, on earth as it is in heaven.
Give us this day our daily bread.
And forgive us our trespasses
as we forgive those who trespass against us.
And lead us not into temptation,
but deliver us from evil.
For thine is the kingdom, the power, and the glory,
for ever and ever. Amen, amen.

The Lord's Prayer

204

1 Our Fa - ther who art in hea - ven,
2 On earth as it is in hea - ven,
3 give us all our tres - pass - es,
4 lead us not in - to temp - ta - tion,
5 thine is the king - dom, the power and the glo - ry,
6 men, a - men, a - - men, a - men,

hal - low - ed a - be thy name, thy king - dom come, thy ___
give us this day our ___
as we for - give those who
but de - li - ver us from ___
for ev - er and ev - er, for
a - men, a - men, a -

Music: Caribbean traditional melody
notated by Olive Pattison
arranged by Harry Grindle (1935–2013)

Words: Caribbean traditional, based on the Lord's Prayer
as taken down by Olive Pattison

205

Auld lang syne

Our Fa - ther, who art in hea - ven, hal-lowed be thy name. Thy

king-dom come, thy _ will be done on _ earth _ as in heav'n. Give

us to-day our _ dai - ly bread and _ for - give our _
lead us not to the time of trial, but de - li - ver us from

sins, ___ as we for-give each one of those who sins ___ a-gainst
e - vil, for thine ___ is the _ king - dom, the _ power _ and the

Music: Scottish traditional melody
arranged by Paul Field (*b.* 1954) and Stephen Deal

born in love a-gain; let all the world sing with one voice, let the peo-ple say 'A-men'.

1   Our Father, who art in heaven,
hallowed be thy name.
Thy kingdom come,
thy will be done
on earth as in heaven.
Give us today our daily bread
and forgive our sins,
as we forgive each one of those
who sins against us;
and lead us not to the time of trial
but deliver us from evil,
for thine is the kingdom,
the power and the glory.

(Repeat verse 1)

2   Let all the people say 'Amen'
in every tribe and tongue;
let every heart's desire be joined
to see the kingdom come.
Let every hope and every dream be born
in love again;
let all the world sing with one voice,
let the people say 'Amen'.

Paul Field (*b.* 1954) and Stephen Deal

206

Lamb of God, you take a-way the sin of the world, have mer-cy on us.

Lamb of God, you take a-way the sin of the world, grant us peace.

It is intended that this setting be sung unaccompanied.

Words: Liturgical text, ELLC

Music: arranged by Peter Thompson (*b.* 1979)
based on Agnus Dei *Cum Iubilo*

207

Lamb of God, you take a-way the sin of the world, have mer-cy on us. Lamb of God, you take a-way the sin of the world, grant us peace.

Words: Liturgical text, ELLC

Music: Lucien Deiss, CSSp (1921–2007)

208

1,2 Lamb of God, you take a-way the sin of the world,

have mer-cy on us, have mer-cy on us.

3 Lamb of God, you take a-way the sin of the world,

grant us peace, grant us peace.

grant us, grant us peace, O grant us peace.

grant us peace, grant us peace.

Words: Liturgical text

Music: Michael Joncas (b. 1951)

209

Ar hyd y nos 84 84 88 84

Lamb of God, you take a-way the sins of the
world. In your mer-cy, come and heal us; Lord, hear our
prayer. Take a-way our sins, for-give us,
Lamb of God, re-store, re-deem us, grant us peace, Lord,

Music: Welsh traditional melody
arranged by Colin Hand (b. 1929)

in   your mer - cy,   Lord,   hear   our   prayer.

Lamb of God, you take away the sins of the world.
In your mercy come and heal us;
Lord, hear our prayer.
Take away our sins, forgive us,
Lamb of God, restore, redeem us,
grant us peace, Lord, in your mercy,
Lord, hear our prayer.

Nick Fawcett (*b.* 1957)

210

Urbs fortitudinis LM

Alternative tune: WAREHAM, *CH5* no. 539

Music: Donald Davison (1937–2013)

Urbs Fortitudinis

1 A city strong we claim as ours,
   salvation seen in walls and towers.
      Fling wide the gates! the way prepare
      for faithful hearts to enter there.

2 Our hearts and minds on God be stayed
   in perfect peace, and undismayed;
      we look to him whose will is best
      and in the Rock of Ages rest.

3 His righteous rule is still the same
   and all our hopes are in his Name:
      he guides our steps, his word we trust,
      and walk with him whose ways are just.

4 To God the Father praise belongs,
   to God the Son we lift our songs:
      with God the Spirit, One in Three,
      to God shall endless glory be.

Timothy Dudley-Smith (*b.* 1926)
based on the Canticle *Urbs Fortitudinis*

211

Music: John Harper
based on South African *Amen Siyakadumisa*

LITURGICAL SECTION

Words: Pentecostal Alleluia

212

Celtic alleluia

Music: Fintan O'Carroll (1922–1981) and Christopher Walker (b. 1947)

Turn over for verses.

1 Fa - ther we praise you as Lord,_____ all of the

earth gives you wor-ship, for your ma - jes-ty____ fills the

Alleluia, alleluia. Alleluia, alleluia.

1 Father, we praise you as Lord,
   all of the earth gives you worship,
   for your majesty fills the heavens, fills the earth.

2 Blessèd apostles sing praise;
   prophets and martyrs give glory:
   'for your majesty, praise the Spirit, praise the Son!'

3 You are the Christ everlasting
   born for us all of a virgin,
   you have conquered death, opened heaven to all believers.

4 Help those you saved by your blood,
   raise them to life with your martyrs.
   Save your people, Lord, as their ruler raise them up.

Fintan O'Carroll (1922–1981)
and Christopher Walker (b. 1947)
based on the Canticle *Te Deum laudamus*

213

Gospel greeting

* The Refrain is first sung by the Cantor, then repeated by All.
  The verses may be sung by the Cantor or Choir.

Music: **Bernadette Farrell** (*b.* 1957)

(Advent) Pre - pare a way for the Lord. _____ Make God's path -
(Christmas) To - day a Sa-viour is born _____ who is Christ
(Easter) Re - joice and sing, all the earth, _____ for the night

-way straight, _____ and all the earth _____ shall see the
the Lord. _____ God's Word is with us and lives a -
is gone! _____ Our God has raised _____ us up from

sav - ing love of _____ God. _____
-mong us with - in _____ our _____ world. _____
death in Christ Je - - - - sus the Son. _____

Words: Bernadette Farrell (b. 1957)

214

Be - hold the Lamb of God, be - -hold the Lamb of God. He takes a - way the sin, the sin of the world.

Be - hold the Lamb, the Lamb of God. He takes a - way the sin of the world.

Behold the Lamb of God,
behold the Lamb of God,
he takes away the sin,
the sin of the world.

John L. Bell (b. 1949)
and Graham Maule (b. 1958)
based on John 1:29

Music: John L. Bell (b. 1949)

215

Venite

1   Come, and let us praise the Lord, *alleluia.*
    He's our God and we are his, *alleluia.*

2   Come to him with songs of praise, *alleluia.*
    Songs of praise, rejoice in him, *alleluia.*

3   For the Lord is a mighty God, *alleluia.*
    He is King of all the world, *alleluia.*

4   In his hands are valleys deep, *alleluia.*
    In his hands are mountain peaks, *alleluia.*

5   In his hands are all the seas, *alleluia.*
    And the lands which he has made, *alleluia.*

6   Praise the Father, praise the Son, *alleluia.*
    Praise the Spirit, the Holy One, *alleluia.*

Anonymous
based on the Canticle *Venite*

Music: African-American traditional melody
    arranged by Julie Bell (*b.* 1979)

216

Dona nobis pacem, pacem.
Dona nobis pacem.
Dona nobis pacem.
Dona nobis pacem.
Dona nobis pacem.
Dona nobis pacem.

Grant us peace.

Final petition from *Agnus Dei*

Music: Early 19th-century traditional round

217

Music: Caribbean traditional melody
adapted and arranged by Hal H. Hopson (b. 1933)

THANKS & PRAISE

Verses

1 Praise God in this ho - ly place, ev - ery na - tion,
2 Ev - ery-thing that breathes now praise: sing your songs, let

ev - ery race. Come, make joy - ful mu - sic to the
voi - ces raise.

Lord. _____ Sound the trum - pet, sound it clear.
Play the cym - bals, play the lute;

Sound it for the world to hear. Come, make joy - ful
play the tim - brel, play the flute.

mu - sic to the Lord.

to Refrain

Words: Caribbean traditional refrain
verses by Hal H. Hopson (b. 1933)
based on Psalm 150

218

Ju - bi - la - te De - o. Ju - bi - la - te
De - o. Al - le - lu - ia.

Words: Phrase from Psalm 100

Music: Early 19th-century traditional round

219

Palace Green

87 87 887

Benedicite

1   Let all creation bless the Lord,
       till heaven with praise is ringing.
     Sun, moon, and stars, peal out a chord,
       stir up the angels' singing.
     Sing, wind and rain! Sing, snow and sleet!
     Make music, day, night, cold, and heat:
       exalt the God who made you.

2   All living things upon the earth,
       green fertile hills and mountains,
     sing to the God who gave you birth;
       be joyful, springs and fountains,
     lithe water-life, bright air-borne birds,
     wild roving beasts, tame flocks and herds:
       exalt the God who made you.

3   O men and women everywhere
       lift up a hymn of glory:
     all you who know God's steadfast care,
       tell out salvation's story.
     No tongue be silent; sing your part,
     you humble souls and meek of heart:
       exalt the God who made you.

Carl P. Daw, Jr (*b.* 1944)
based on the Canticle *Benedicite*

Music: Michael Fleming (1928–2006)

220

Stenka Razin

87 87

The tune is sung twice to each verse of words.

Music: Russian folk-song *Ponizovaya Volnitsa*
arranged by Jacqueline Mullen (b. 1961)

Nunc Dimittis

1   Long the years of faithful waiting,
      let your servant go in peace;
   in the temple contemplating,
      longing now for death's release;
   in this child, the adoration
      of the ancient's life of prayer;
   he, this old man's culmination
      trusting to a mother's care.

2   Vision of the Lord's salvation,
      child to set God's people free;
   Israel's hope and consolation,
      ancient eyes salvation see.
   Faithful years of contemplating,
      watchful soul, your cares release;
   faithful in your watch and waiting,
      faithful servant, go in peace.

Paul Gilmore (*b.* 1968)
based on the Canticle *Nunc Dimittis*

These words were written for the tune IN THE GLOAMING, no. 132.

221

Let us pray to the Lord.   Lord, hear our prayer.

Alternate Response: Lord, have mercy.

222

Music: Owen Alstott (b. 1947)

Harmony (optional, upper or lower voices)

Melody

1 My soul pro-claims your might-y deeds. My spi-rit sings the

D.S.

great-ness of your name.

Magnificat

2   Your mercy flows throughout the land
     and every generation knows your love.

3   You cast the mighty from their thrones
     and raise the poor and lowly to new life.

4   You fill the hungry with good things.
     With empty hands you send the rich away.

5   Just as you promised Abraham,
     you come to free your people, Israel.

Owen Alstott (*b.* 1947)
based on the Canticle *Magnificat*

222 Words and Music: © 1984, 1991, Published by OCP, 5536 NE Hassalo, Portland, OR 97213, USA. All rights reserved. Used
with permission.

223

Benedictus

66 888 6

Benedictus

1   Our God and Father bless,
    for by his sworn decree
      he sends to us in power divine
      the promised Lord of David's line,
      fulfilling all his love's design
    to save and set us free.

Music: Theodore P. Saunders (*b.* 1957)

2 His ancient purpose stands,
unchanged for evermore,
   that we and all who find a place
   within his covenant of grace
   may freely come before his face
to worship and adore.

3 Let truth prepare his path,
let righteousness increase!
   that from the shade of nature's night
   to dawn of heaven's glory bright
   the ransomed children of the light
may walk the way of peace.

Timothy Dudley-Smith (b. 1926)
based on the Canticle *Benedictus*

224

Through our lives and by our prayers, your kingdom come.

Through our lives
and by our prayers,
your kingdom come.

John L. Bell (b. 1949)
and Graham Maule (b. 1958)

Music: John L. Bell (b. 1949)

225

Corde natus

87 87 87 7

For another arrangement of this tune see *CH5* no. 175.

1   We believe in God Almighty,
        maker of the earth and sky;
    all we see and all that's hidden
        is his work unceasingly:
    God our Father's loving kindness
        with us till the day we die –
        evermore and evermore.

2   We believe in Christ the Saviour,
        Son of God and Son of Man;
    born of Mary, preaching, healing,
        crucified, yet risen again:
    he ascended to the Father
        there in glory long to reign –
        evermore and evermore.

3   We believe in God the Spirit,
        present in our lives today;
    speaking through the prophets' writings,
        guiding travellers on their way:
    to our hearts he brings forgiveness
        and the hope of endless joy –
        evermore and evermore.

                            David Mowbray (b. 1938)

Music: Piæ Cantiones, 1582
    arranged by Peter Thompson (b. 1979)

226

Stranmillis

87 87 D

Alternative tune: LUX EOI, *CH5* no. 251

1   We believe in God the Father,
        God Almighty, by whose plan
    earth and heaven sprang to being,
        all created things began.
    We believe in Christ the Saviour,
        Son of God in human frame,
    virgin-born, the child of Mary
        upon whom the Spirit came.

2   Christ, who on the cross forsaken,
        like a lamb to slaughter led,
    suffered under Pontius Pilate,
        he descended to the dead.
    We believe in Jesus risen,
        heaven's King to rule and reign,
    to the Father's side ascended
        till as judge he comes again.

3   We believe in God the Spirit;
        in one church, below, above:
    saints of God in one communion,
        one in holiness and love.
    So by faith, our sins forgiven,
        Christ our Saviour, Lord and friend,
    we shall rise with him in glory
        to the life that knows no end.

                    Timothy Dudley-Smith (*b.* 1926)

Music: Harry Grindle (1935–2013)

227

North Bailey

See overleaf music for verses 2, 4.

Alternative tune: ST FULBERT, *CH5* no. 292

Music: Peter Moger (b. 1964)

Magnificat

1   With Mary let my soul rejoice,
        and praise God's holy name –
     his saving love from first to last,
        from age to age, the same!

2   *see overleaf*

3   The rich our God will send away
        and feed the hungry poor;
     the arms of love remain outstretched
        at mercy's open door.

4   *see overleaf*

5   All glory to the Father, Son
        and Spirit now proclaim;
     with Mary let the world rejoice
        and praise God's holy name!

David Mowbray (*b.* 1938)
based on the Canticle *Magnificat*

2   How strong his arm, how great his power!
       the proud he will disown;
  the meek and humble he exalts
      to share his glorious throne.

4   So shall God's promise be fulfilled,
      to Israel firmly made:
  a child is born, a Son is given
      whose crown will never fade.

David Mowbray (*b.* 1938)
based on the Canticle *Magnificat*

CREDAL STRUCTURE OF CONTENTS

CREDAL STRUCTURE OF CONTENTS

The Canticles

Benedicite
219 Let all creation bless the Lord

Benedictus
223 Our God and Father bless

Jubilate
218 Jubilate Deo

Magnificat
222 *My soul rejoices in God, my Saviour*
227 With Mary let my soul rejoice

Nunc Dimittis
220 Long the years of faithful waiting

Urbs Fortitudinis
210 A city strong we claim as ours

Venite
215 Come, and let us praise the Lord, *alleluia*

Other Liturgical Items

Beatitudes
18 Blest are they, the poor in spirit

Benedictions
104 Now go in peace, now go in love
105 Now let your people depart in peace

Exsultet
129 Sing, choirs of heaven! Let saints and angels sing

Prayer attributed to St Francis of Assisi
92 Lord, make us servants of your peace

Seven words from the cross
145 The hour has come, foretold since time began

Stabat Mater
76 Jesus on the cross is dying

Appropriate for children's worship

2 A sign shall be given
3 Advent candles tell their story
7 *Allundé, allundé, allundé alluya*
10 Be bold, be strong
15 *Bless the Lord, O my soul, O my soul*
17 Blessèd is the King who comes
24 Clap your hands all you nations
27 Come, sing the praise of Jesus
30 Don't build your house on the sandy land
33 *Faith as small as a mustard seed*
35 Father God, you love me and you know me inside out
39 Give me peace, O Lord, I pray
44 *God loves you, and I love you*
49 Hallelu, hallelu, hallelu, hallelujah
50 He came down that we may have love
51 He made the stars to shine
52 He's got the whole world in his hands
58 *I will not be afraid of what I hear*
61 I'll go in the strength of the Lord
62 *I'm gonna jump up and down*
69 Jesus, be the centre
74 Jesus lead us to the Father
75 Jesu's love is very wonderful
79 *Joshua fought the battle of Jericho*
82 Let me tell you about a baby
91 Lord, I lift your name on high
96 Mister Noah built an ark
98 My God is so big, so strong and so mighty
108 O God of Faith
117 *Our God is a great big God*
123 See him lying on a bed of straw
124 See the Lamb of God
128 Sing a song, sing a joyful song
139 Stop and think, don't be so fast
141 Tagaimis le chéile os comhair an Rí
143 *Teach me to dance to the beat of your heart*
147 The Lord's my shepherd *(Townend)*
149 The virgin Mary had a baby boy
152 *This little light of mine, I'm gonna let it shine*
165 Who is the Rock?
167 With Jesus in the boat
168 Wonderful Lord, wonderful God
171 You are my strength when I am weak
172 You can't stop rain from falling down
195 *Gloria in excelsis Deo (Anderson)*
204 Our Father *(Caribbean)*
205 Our Father *(Millenium Prayer)*
215 Come, and let us praise the Lord, *alleluia*
217 *Halle, halle, hallelujah!*

INDEX OF BIBLICAL REFERENCES

INDEX OF BIBLICAL REFERENCES

INDEX OF BIBLICAL REFERENCES

THANKS & PRAISE

THANKS & PRAISE

8: 35-37   O Church arise, and put your armour on   107

INDEX OF BIBLICAL REFERENCES

INDEX OF BIBLICAL REFERENCES

INDEX OF AUTHORS, TRANSLATORS
AND SOURCES OF TEXTS

INDEX OF COMPOSERS, ARRANGERS AND SOURCES OF TUNES

ALPHABETICAL INDEX OF TUNES

METRICAL INDEX OF TUNES

INDEX OF FIRST LINES AND TUNES

Addresses of principal copyright holders

Representative Church Body (RCB)
Church of Ireland House, Church Avenue, Rathmines, Dublin 6
<office@rcbdub.org>

Association for Promoting of Christian Knowledge (APCK)
Church of Ireland House, Church Avenue, Rathmines, Dublin 6
<apck@ireland.anglican.org>

GIA
GIA Publications Inc., 7404 S. Mason Avenue, Chicago, IL 60638, USA

Hope Publishing Company
Carol Stream, IL 60188, USA

Jubilate Hymns
The Jubilate Group, Kitley House, St Katherines Road,
Torquay TQ1 4DE <copyrightmanager@jubilate.co.uk>

Kingsway Music
26-28 Lottbridge Drove, Eastbourne, East Sussex BN23 6NT, UK

Kevin Mayhew
Buxhall, Stowmarket, Suffolk IP14 3BW, UK

Music Sales Ltd
14-15 Berners Street, London W1T 3LJ, UK

OCP Publications
5536 NE Hassalo, Portland, OR 97213, USA

Oxford University Press
Great Clarendon Street, Oxford OX2 6DP, UK

Song Solutions
14 Horsted Square, Uckfield, East Sussex, TN22 1QG,
United Kingdom. <info@songsolutions.org>

Stainer & Bell Ltd
PO Box 110, Victoria House, 23 Gruneisen Road,
London N3 1DZ, UK <post@stainer.co.uk>

Ateliers et Presses de Taizé
71250 Taizé-Community, France

continued overleaf

Thankyou Music
Administered (UK and Europe) by Kingsway Music *(see above)*
<tym@kingsway.co.uk>

Wild Goose Resource Group (WGRG)
4th Floor, Savoy Centre, 140 Sauchiehall Street, Glasgow G2 3DH
<admin@iona.org.uk>

Licensing bodies:

Christian Copyright Licensing International
CCLI (UK and Ireland)
Chantry House, 22 Upperton Road, Eastbourne BN21 1BF, UK
Contact form at <uk.ccli.com/contact/>

Calamus (UK and Ireland)
Decani Music Ltd, Oak House, 70 High Street, Brandon, IP27 0AU,
UK

Note by Wild Goose Resource Group:
Local Church and Educational use of WGRG material is covered by
CCLI (Christian Copyright Licensing) and Calamus. If your church
or school holds a licence for either of these licensing schemes, please
report usage of WGRG materials in your church or school's annual
reporting.